A. C. Hervey

The Books of Chronicles in Relation to the Pentateuch and the Higher Criticism

A. C. Hervey

The Books of Chronicles in Relation to the Pentateuch and the Higher Criticism

ISBN/EAN: 9783337159542

Printed in Europe, USA, Canada, Australia, Japan

Cover: Foto ©Lupo / pixelio.de

More available books at **www.hansebooks.com**

The Books of Chronicles in relation to the Pentateuch and the "*Higher Criticism.*"

FIVE LECTURES DELIVERED BEFORE THE "SOCIETY FOR
PROMOTING HIGHER RELIGIOUS EDUCATION"
AT WELLS, IN THE SPRING OF 1892

BY LORD A. C. HERVEY, D.D.

BISHOP OF BATH AND WELLS

PUBLISHED UNDER THE DIRECTION OF THE TRACT COMMITTEE.

LONDON:
SOCIETY FOR PROMOTING CHRISTIAN KNOWLEDGE,
NORTHUMBERLAND AVENUE, W.C., 43, QUEEN VICTORIA STREET, E.C.
BRIGHTON: 135, NORTH STREET.
NEW YORK: E. & J. B. YOUNG & CO.
1892.

CONTENTS.

	PAGE
PREFATORY NOTE	5

LECTURE I.

THEORY OF THE "HIGHER CRITICISM" WITH REGARD TO THE PENTATEUCH, AND THE HISTORICAL BOOKS OF THE OLD TESTAMENT 7

LECTURE II.

THEORY OF THE "HIGHER CRITICISM" WITH REGARD TO THE PENTATEUCH (*continued*) . . . 44

LECTURE III.

MISCELLANEOUS REMARKS ON THE EARLIER BOOKS OF THE OLD TESTAMENT, AND THEIR AUTHENTICITY . 83

LECTURE IV.

THE BOOKS OF CHRONICLES 112

LECTURE V.

CONCLUSIVE TESTIMONY OF CHRONICLES TO THE MOSAIC LAW 141

PREFATORY NOTE.

My object in the ensuing course of Lectures is two-fold: first, to give you such information with regard to the Books of Chronicles as it is in my power to do, with a view of showing the authenticity and historical trustworthiness of the Books; and secondly, to enable you by the help of such information to form an independent judgment upon some of the conclusions come to by what is known by the name of the "Higher Criticism."

LIST OF BOOKS CHIEFLY USED IN THE FOLLOWING LECTURES.

WELLHAUSEN'S *Prolegomena to the History of Israel.* (English translation.)

KUENEN'S *Hexateuch.* (English translation.)

DRIVER'S *Introduction to the Literature of the Old Testament.*

W. SMITH'S *The Pentateuch.*

WRIGHT'S *Empire of the Hittites.*

BISHOP OF GLOUCESTER AND BRISTOL, *Christus Comprobator.*

STANLEY LEATHES, *The Law in the Prophets.*

SAYCE, *Fresh Light from the Monuments.*

KINNS, *Graven in the Rock.*

HERVEY'S *Genealogies of our Lord.*

LEPSIUS' *Egypt, Ethiopia, and Sinai.*

Dictionary of the Bible, Articles — 'Kings and Chronicles.'

LECTURE I.

Theory of the "Higher Criticism" with regard to the Pentateuch, and the Historical Books of the Old Testament.

The "Higher Criticism" is a system of critical analysis by which the critic professes to be able to take the Books of Scripture which have come down to us in a certain traditional form—known as the Canon of the Old Testament—and to break them up into their component parts. In sifting and separating these parts he determines by the light of his own intelligence which of them have any historical truth at all in them, which have none; he determines the age when each was written, and the exact motives of each writer in the statements which he makes; when there is any historical truth at the bottom of any statement, the critic produces such truth in the form in which it really happened three or four thousand years ago, and explains to you the motives of the writer in presenting it to the reader in the widely different form in which it has been received as history through successive ages. These motives are sometimes comparatively innocent, as e.g. when a false name, such as that of Moses, is assigned to certain useful laws to give weight and authority to them; but sometimes they are purely corrupt, as when interested priests write spurious histories like the Books of Chronicles for the purpose of enhancing their own dignity and securing their own emoluments.

The results obtained by the exercise of these ample critical powers are as follows: The history in our Bibles from Genesis to the close of the Hexateuch—i.e. the Pentateuch *plus* the Book of Joshua—is made up of the following materials. First the Elohistic narrative, which deals mainly with legislation strung together on a framework of narrative. This part is distinguished by its use of the word *Elohim* for God. With this is combined the Jehovistic story-book, including the history of the Patriarchs. This part is distinguished by the use of the name *Jehovah* (LORD, A. V.) for God. But this division does not meet all the exigencies of the case. A third writer has to be invented, who partakes of some of the characteristics of both the Jehovist and the Elohist. These three contributors to the Bible History are distinguished by the letters E, J, and JE. A fourth and fifth or sixth is the Deuteronomist (whose work is quite separate, and whose connection with Moses is purely imaginary) and others who write in his spirit, marked by the letter D, D^1, and D^2. But the combined labours of E and J and JE and the D's, did not come into their present shape at once. We have to distinguish as separate works (1) the Priestly Code, comprising Leviticus, and the allied portions of Exodus and Numbers, and this again is subdivided into P^1, P^2, P^3, &c., according as they wrote in the priestly spirit. (2) The Book of the covenant, comprising Exod. xxi–xxiii, and other passages relating to covenants represented by Q, meaning 4. (3) Deuteronomy, and according to some, a Book of Holiness. It is also thought that some other fragments and interpolations may have gone to make up the whole. And then finally there is R, the Redactor or editor of the whole Hexateuch, and successive Redactors known as R^2, R^3, &c. As regards the very important question of the age of these different documents, though some difference of opinion still exists among the leading critics, there is considerable consensus on the following heads:—

1. The Book of Deuteronomy, or the bulk of

it, was really composed in the reign of Josiah, when Hilkiah, the High Priest, pretended to have found it in the Temple, some seven centuries after the death of Moses.

2. The Priestly Code, which comprises the great bulk of what has been commonly known as the Mosaic or Levitical law, with its whole round of sacrifice, priesthood, central sanctuary, one altar, and so on, dates from later still, about B.C. 445. It is the work of the Exilic period, and was first put into action by concert between Ezra and Nehemiah. Its whole apparatus of a movable Tabernacle, wandering camp, and other archaic details, with its legislation strictly confined to the situation in the wilderness, were so skilfully contrived to conceal its true date, that it has passed as genuine history till the "Higher Criticism" arose to detect the imposture (Introduction, Wellhausen, p. 9).

3. The Jehovistic narrative, comprising the rest of the history of the Israelitish people down to the occupation of Canaan, was composed for the most part in the time of the Assyrian monarchy, with the help of tradition and some old documents.

4. To the same age belong the other historical Books—Judges, Samuel, and Kings. But these have not been allowed to come down to us in

their original state. "A revision of them much more thorough than is commonly assumed" took place towards the end of the Babylonian exile (Wellhausen, Introd., p. 8), in other words, the redactors of the Exilic period made the ancient Books tell the story of the sixth or seventh century before Christ, instead of that of the thirteenth, twelfth, or tenth, as the case might be.

5. The Books of Chronicles belong to the beginning of the Greek domination (p. 294) after B.C. 330. In them the writer, a Priest, or Levite, has transformed the whole history so as to square with the Priests' Code, and make it appear that the so-called Mosaic legislation had existed all through the times from Saul to the return from the Babylonish Captivity. Among other things he formed fictitious genealogies, to support his views of the Aaronic Priesthood, and the Levitical institutions.

Such are some of the main results reached by this "Higher Criticism" as set forth chiefly in the work of Wellhausen on "the History of Israel," and Kuenen on "the Hexateuch." It is obvious to remark that it revolutionizes the received views of Holy Scripture as "given by Inspiration of God," and degrades the books of the Old Testament not only to the level of fallible human writings, but to that of wilfully false and misleading history; and this it does without one particle of historical evidence to support it.

Nor is it only the Old Testament which is affected by this destructive criticism. The Old Testament is the foundation on which the New Testament is built. The credit of our Lord and His apostles is pledged to the truth of the Scriptures. The Lord Jesus tells us Himself that He came to fulfil the law; that Moses wrote of Him; that all things must be fulfilled which were written in the law of Moses, and in the Prophets, and in the Psalms concerning Him; that the Scripture cannot be broken: with numerous similar sayings. The apostles all speak in the same strain. They speak of the death and resurrection of Jesus Christ as the necessary fulfilment of what God had showed by the mouth of His Prophets. St. Paul in all his Epistles refers to the " Holy Scriptures," to " the law," to " the oracles of God," to " the covenants and the giving of the law," to " Moses," to the giving of the law " 430 years after the promise to Abraham," and always treats the Holy Scriptures as authorities of absolute veracity and trustworthiness. The Epistle to the Hebrews dwells largely on the mission of Moses, on the respective Priesthoods of Aaron and Jesus Christ, on the spiritual significance of the

Tabernacle, and various parts of the Mosaic ceremonial. And, in a word, the whole teaching of the New Testament is founded upon the truth and authenticity and divine authority of the Holy Scriptures as we have received them from the Jews. The theory therefore of the "Higher Criticism" not only affects our estimate of the Scriptures of the Old Testament, but also shakes to its very foundations the fabric of New Testament doctrine which rests upon the Old.

In particular there is one way in which the "Higher Criticism" affects the doctrine of Christ, which is too important, too momentous, to be passed over in silence. It is admitted on all hands that our Lord Jesus Christ taught plainly and unreservedly the divine authority and Mosaic authorship of the Books traditionally ascribed to him (e. g. Matt. v. 17, 18, xix. 8, xxii. 31, 32, xxiii. 2 ; Mark x. 9, xii. 26 ; Luke xvi. 31, xx. 37 ; xxiv. 26, 27, 44 ; John iii. 14, v. 45, 46, 47, vi. 32, 49, vii. 19, 22, &c.). Hence those who accept the teaching of the "Higher Criticism" with regard to the Pentateuch are reduced to the painful alternative of believing either that our Lord taught what He knew not to be true, or that He shared the ignorance of the men of His own generation, and believed that to be true which the brighter light of the "Higher Criticism" has since discovered to be false. The English school of critics has for the most part adopted the latter alternative, and though they endeavour to minimize the evil by speaking of the questions at issue as mere *literary questions,* and on the other hand by speaking of the "limitation of our Lord's knowledge" as "self-imposed," and as a part of the κένωσις (kenosis), or self-emptying of His Divine Glory which was a necessary part (they say) of the Incarnation (Phil. ii. 7), yet the broad fact remains that the Lord Jesus, the Teacher sent from God, to whom St. Peter said, Lord, thou knowest all things; in whom dwelleth the fullness of the Godhead bodily; in whom are hid all the treasures of wisdom and knowledge; to whom the Father gave the Spirit not by measure; who spake the Words of God; to whom the Father showeth all things that Himself doeth; was not merely passively nescient of how the Father had dealt with the chosen race in the ages past, but actively taught, in the fulfilment of His Divine mission, that which has since been proved to be false by the wisdom of the "Higher Critics."

Obviously therefore the conclusions with regard to the Old Testament Scriptures arrived at by the "Higher Criticism" are matters affecting very seriously the vital interests of Christianity and of the Church of God. It is not too much to say that no danger of an equally threatening character and subversive tendency has appeared in the Church during the many centuries of her existence.

Still, had the "Higher Criticism" been confined to the regions of its birth in Germany, it might have been wise to leave it alone to perish by the law of its own origin, and after the example of its many predecessors in the regions of speculative theology. It is a different matter now that these speculations are taken up by grave English Divines, and are fostered in our English Universities. When the columns of both the leading secular and religious newspapers are filled with correspondence on "the Bible and modern criticism," when the pages of our magazines and reviews contain numerous articles advocating and supporting the new views, and when the press is teeming with publications on either side of the controversy, it is no longer possible for ordinary Christians to remain in peaceful ignorance of the strife which is raging around them. It becomes the duty therefore of every educated Churchman or Churchwoman to know something of the grounds on which belief in the Old Testament Scriptures rests, and to be in possession of some rational and valid arguments for rejecting decisively views, from whatever quarter they may proceed, which destroy confidence in the Bible as the revealed word of God. And it is, I think, a proper function of our "Society for promoting higher religious education" to endeavour to supply such arguments, and to set the minds of its members at rest on matters so deeply affecting the faith of Christendom.

I propose therefore in the ensuing course of Lectures first to lay before you some of the chief grounds, as far as my information goes, on which the "Higher Criticism" rests its demands on all Christian people to give up their belief in the Pentateuch as in any true sense a faithful record of the work and words of Moses, and a trustworthy historical record of God's dealings with the Israelitish people. And after each such statement I shall endeavour to expose step by step the utter insufficiency of each of these alleged grounds to bear the conclusions which are built upon them; and in some cases I shall rebut what are absolutely false statements by clear historical evidence to the contrary. This will occupy our *two* first Lectures.

Our *third* Lecture will contain a general view of the historical books of the Old Testament, their composition, their unity, their historical accuracy, the transparent honesty of the writers, the evidence of the ages to their unimpeachable veracity.

Our *fourth* and *fifth* Lectures will deal directly with the first and second Books of Chronicles.

In trying to lay before you the chief grounds on which the " Higher Criticism " impugns the authenticity and historical character of the Pentateuch, I shall not attempt to follow Wellhausen in his running fire of profane banter, and utterly frivolous objections to the manner in which things are stated, and his attempts to make out contradictions and inconsistencies where none exist. His method of treating the history as a collection of myths, some earlier and some later, and of dealing with the myths relating to the earlier ages, as really the product of the civilization of the later times to which he relegates the writers who recorded them, is utterly destructive of any real philosophical treatment of the books, and simply turns them upside down. But I shall collect under a few heads the chief objections of weight, as far as I know them, that have been brought forward by different scholars, such as Bishop Colenso, Dr. Davidson, Wellhausen, Kuenen, and others, against the traditional view of the Pentateuch being in the main the work of Moses, and a faithful reporter of the events recorded in it. These heads are as follows:

I. Contradictions and inconsistencies in the several narratives betraying their composite nature as the work of different writers, and representing the ideas of very different ages from that to which they profess to belong.

II. Anachronisms, showing that the writer lived long after Moses.

III. That the Hebrew of the Pentateuch is not the Hebrew of the age of Moses, but of much later ages; and also that many words and phrases betray the fact that the people had long been living in Canaan when such passages were written.

IV. That the Pentateuch betrays a much higher state of civilization than could have existed at so early an age.

V. That there is no evidence of the existence of the Mosaic Institutions, between the time of the Exodus, when the Mosaic laws purport to have been given, and the later times of the Jewish monarchy; and that in point of fact the moveable Tabernacle, the Aaronic Priesthood, the Levitical order, the one place of sacrifice, are all late inventions, with which Moses had nothing whatever to do, and which were unknown till many centuries after his death.

These are, I believe, the most weighty arguments of the "Higher Criticism," and I proceed to develop them as I find them in the books of the "Higher Critics," and to deal with them one by one, to the best of my ability.

I. It is alleged that there is a contradiction between the account of the Creation given in Gen. i.–ii. 3, the work of the Elohist, and that given in Gen. ii. 4–25, the work of the Jehovist. That whereas in the first the vegetable and animal world are created before man, and man comes into being last, in the second (Gen. ii. 4–25) man is created before the vegetable world, and the animals were created after man was planted in the garden of Eden, and brought to him to see whether among them there was any one meet to be a companion for man, and that when none such was found then woman was made. Now is there one word of truth in this statement? Any one who is familiar with the narratives of the Old Testament must have observed how frequent a method it is with the Old Testament writers to give first a general narrative, and then to go back and give the details of any particular part of the preceding narratives which it is desired to record. Thus Gen. xi. 31 gives the general statement of Abraham's departure with his father Terah from Ur of the Chaldees to Haran. But Gen. xii. 1 goes back to add the important detail that God had appeared to him in Ur, and bid him leave his father's house and go to the land of Canaan. In Gen. xxxvii. 5 we read "Joseph dreamed a dream, and he told it his brethren: and they hated him yet the more;" and then follows the dream in verses 6 and 7. In 1 Sam. xvi. 21 we read of David coming to Saul to play to him when the evil spirit was upon him, and that he became Saul's armour-bearer. But ch. xvii. goes back and relates the combat with Goliath, which was the immediate cause of his becoming Saul's armour-bearer, and abiding permanently at Saul's court. Numerous other instances are scattered through the pages of the Old Testament. In accordance, then, with this common method of Hebrew narrative, it is very natural that the history of creation, after the general comprehensive narrative of ch. i., should go back to supply certain details which it was desirable to add. And that this is the character of ch. ii. 4-25, and that it has ch. i. in view all the time, is evident from the repetition in ch. ii. of the different phrases of ch. i. Compare ii. 4 with i. 1 and ii. 3; and ii. 5 with i. 11, 12; and ii. 19, 20 with i. 20-26; and ii. 20-23 with i. 27.

I would also observe that if there are two possible interpretations of the meaning of a passage in any book, even if it be a book of Scripture, one of which is in direct contradiction of other statements of that book, and the other is in harmony with them, it is the dictate of common sense and of sound criticism to accept the interpretation which agrees with those other undoubted statements, and not the one which disagrees with them.

Looking then at Gen. ii. 5 foll. we find that the writer goes back to three heads which had been summarily related in the preceding chapter, viz. the creation of the vegetable world, of the animal world, and of man, with the view of adding certain details which the progress of the history of man, now placed in the garden of Eden, seemed to require. He therefore mentions first the interesting fact [1] that for a length of time the growth of herb and tree could not take place because there was no rain. Neither, he adds, was there a man to till the ground. But both these wants were in due time supplied (ver. 9). And this gives occasion

---

[1] There are two ways of translating ver. 5, that of the Authorised Version, which in this follows the Septuagint, and that of the Revised Version. But the difference does not affect the question before us.

to add, for the first time, the very important statement concerning man, that he was formed out of the dust of the ground [1]. But there was another detail to be supplied concerning man. Gen. i. 29 had merely stated generally "male and female created He them." But how the woman was created, whether simultaneously or otherwise, no hint was given. This information, with its far-spreading social consequences (v. 23–25; 1 Cor. xi. 3–12; 1 Tim. ii. 12–15), was now to be given. As soon as the man was set in the garden of Eden it was evident that it was not good for him to be alone. "I will make him a help meet for him," said the Lord God. And what immediately gave rise to the expression of this divine purpose was the transaction recorded in vv. 19, 20. In accordance with that sovereignty of man over the whole animal creation which had been asserted in Gen. i. 26–28, the Lord brought every beast of the field, and every fowl of the air, which He had made, before Adam that he might name them. And Adam gave them all names.

Incidentally this parade of the animals revealed the fact that in spite of all the various

---

[1] The Hebrew for *man* is *adam*; for the *ground* is *adamah*; so in Latin, *Homo* is *man* (humanus); *Humus* is the *ground*.

qualities possessed by various animals—strength, and beauty, and swiftness, and sagacity, and industry, and so on, not one was a help meet for man. For not one was created in the image of God, and so God said " I will make him an help meet for him." And then follows the mysterious account of the formation of the woman out of man.

That there is any contradiction or inconsistency between the accounts of Creation given in the first and second chapters of Genesis is absolutely untrue.

Passing over divers frivolous objections to the story of Jacob and Esau, to the history of Joseph (usually considered a perfect model of narrative, but in which Wellhausen doubts whether there is any historical basis), and in which Dr. Driver sees manifold proofs of the mixture of two different accounts, we will glance for a moment at the account of the institution of the Passover given in Exod. xii. Dr. Driver tells us in p. 26 of his Introduction to the Old Testament that " the inference is *irresistible* that Exod. xii. 21–27 is part of a different account of the institution of the Passover" from that contained in xii. 1–20, or rather, xii. 1–13, because he strangely says " xii. 14–20 do not concern the Passover at all."

Now what are the reasons for this inference which it is impossible to resist? "The verses 21–27 do not describe the execution of the commands received by Moses in vv. 1–13." "Moses does not repeat to the people the injunctions received by him." "Several points of importance, e.g. the character of the lamb, and the manner in which it was to be eaten, are omitted." "Fresh points, the hyssop, the basin, none to leave the house ... are added." Now let us see whether vv. 21–27 do or do not describe the execution of the commands received by Moses. Verse 3 says, "Speak ye unto all the congregation of Israel, saying, In the tenth day of this month they shall take to them every man a lamb, according to the house of their fathers." In ver. 21, "Then Moses called for all the elders of Israel, and said unto them, Draw out and take you a lamb according to your families, and kill the Passover." Verse 7 says, "And they shall take of the blood, and strike it on the two side posts, and on the upper door post of the houses, wherein they shall eat it." Verse 22 says, "And ye shall take a bunch of hyssop, and dip it in the blood that is in the bason, and strike the lintel and the two side posts with the blood that is in the bason; and none of you shall go out of the door of his house until the morning."

Verse 12 says, "For I will pass through the land of Egypt this night, and will smite all the first-born in the land of Egypt, both man and beast." Verse 23 says, "For the Lord will pass through to smite the Egyptians." Verse 13 says, "And the blood shall be to you for a token upon the houses where ye are: and when I see the blood I will pass over you, and the plague shall not be upon you to destroy you." Verse 23 says, "And when He seeth the blood upon the lintel, and on the two side posts, the Lord will pass over the door, and will not suffer the destroyer to come in unto your houses to smite you[1]." I affirm, then, that the inference is irresistible in a directly contrary direction to that spoken of by Dr. Driver; and that unless it is an axiom that when A gives instructions to B to be delivered to C, and the history relates such delivery, and goes on to describe the performance by C of the instructions so delivered, the narrator must, if he is a true man, repeat verbatim the exact terms of the instructions three times, 1st as given by A, 2nd as delivered by B, and 3rdly as performed by C.—I say

[1] It may be worth noticing the identity of the Hebrew root for *plague* in ver. 13, with that of the verb to *smite* in ver. 23. And also the agreement in ver. 28 of the mention of "Moses and Aaron" with the plur. of ver. 3.

unless this is an axiom, the inference from the points of agreement enumerated above is "*irresistible*," that we have before us one consistent and consecutive account of the Institution of the Passover, and have no need of the help of E or J, or JE, or any of the P's or D's, or any one else, to clear up matters and set them straight.

Other contradictions or inconsistencies, betraying a dual authorship, are alleged between some of the laws in Deuteronomy and those in other parts of the Pentateuch. Some of these variations, as e. g. greater insistence on the One Place where the Festivals were to be kept, and sacrifices offered (compare Deut. xxi. 6, 16 with Exod. xxiii. 14), are so manifestly caused by the greater proximity in time and place to the occupation of Canaan when the laws of Deuteronomy were given, compared with the time and place of the giving of the earlier laws, that we need not stop to dwell on them. Others, as e. g. the silence of Deuteronomy about the year of jubilee, apparent differences about the law of tithes in Deut. xiv. and Num. xviii., may possibly indicate in some cases additions or modifications in particular laws in the course of ages. But they are absolutely imponderable when weighed with the solid mass of harmonious agreement. I will therefore only take into consideration one case of difference which has been made a good deal of. I mean the version of the ten commandments as given in Deut. v. as compared with that given in Exod. xx. If you place these two versions of the ten commandments side by side, you will see that the chief difference is in the fourth commandment. In Exod. xx., after the enacting clause prohibiting labour on the Sabbath day for all, down to "thy stranger that is within thy gates," there follows the reason for this sanctity of the seventh day, viz. "For in six days the Lord made heaven and earth," and so on.

But in Deut. v., after the same enacting clause as above, "nor the stranger that is within thy gates," instead of the reference to the six days' creation, and the rest on the seventh day, there follows, "that thy manservant and thy maidservant may rest as well as thou. And remember that thou wast a servant in the land of Egypt, and that the Lord thy God brought thee out thence through a mighty hand and by a stretched out arm: therefore the Lord thy God commandeth thee to keep the Sabbath day." Now it seems to me that nothing can be more natural under the circumstances than such variation. According to the narrative in Deuteronomy Moses is *not here legislating*. He is recalling to the memory of his hearers the legislation given at Sinai. The law of the ten commandments "written and engraven on stones" was actually among them (Deut. x. 5). In referring to it *memoriter*, he added a comment of his own to enforce it, using the same words as are recorded in Exod. xxiii. 12. The whole thing is so natural that I cannot imagine anybody seeing any difficulty in it.

It is not necessary to pursue this part of the subject further. The above are only intended as specimens of the kind of contradictions alleged by the "Higher Criticism." They tell us, it is true, that their arguments are *cumulative*. But no number of arguments, each of which is improbable in itself, can make up a total probability, any more than any number of minus quantities can make up an integral quantity. I venture to think that there is absolutely nothing in the cases we have considered to throw the slightest suspicion upon the authenticity of the books before us.

II. The second head of objections, that of the existence of anachronisms in the Pentateuch, showing that the writer lived long after Moses, is, at first sight, much more serious, inasmuch

IN RELATION TO THE PENTATEUCH. 29

as the objections rest upon facts, and not upon mere fancies. Let us look honestly and boldly at the principal ones.

(*a*) Gen. xii. 6, "And the Canaanite was then in the land." And xiii. 7, "The Canaanite and the Perizzite dwelled then in the land." These passages have often been adduced as proofs that Genesis was written after the destruction of the Canaanites. But on the whole they seem rather to refer to Gen. x. 18, 19, and to mean that the settlement of the Canaanites in the land of Canaan had already taken place.

(*b*) Gen. xxxvi. 31–39, "These are the kings of Edom that reigned in the land of Edom, before there reigned any king over the children of Israel." Here is a distinct mention of Kings of Israel, and so a distinct proof that this passage was written after there were Kings in Israel. Moreover, the genealogy of the Kings of Edom here given goes down to the time of Saul the first king of Israel.

(*c*) Another instance is found in Gen. xiv. 14, when we read that Abraham pursued the kings "unto Dan." And in Deut. xxxiv. 1 that the Lord showed Moses "all the land of Gilead, unto Dan." But we read in Judg. xviii. 10 that the ancient name of the city was Laish, and that the name was changed to Dan, by the

Danites who took possession of it in the days of the Judges, long after the death of Moses. See, too, Num. xiv. 45; xxi. 3; Deut. i. 44, compared with Judg. i. 17 for the parallel case of Hormah.

(*d*) In Num. xxxii. 40-43, we read that Moses gave Gilead to Machir the son of Manasseh, and that Jair the son of Manasseh, took the small towns thereof, and called them Havoth-Jair, i. e. the villages of Jair. In Deut. iii. 14 this information is repeated, but with the addition "unto this day," words which are repeated in Judg. x. 4, but which seem out of place with reference to an event which had taken place only a few months before, and to imply a duration of many years (cp. Josh. iv. 9; Judg. i. 26; 2 Sam. vii. 6; 1 Kings viii. 9) during which they were still known as Havoth-Jair.

(*e*) Deut. xxxiv. 10, "There arose not a prophet since in Israel like unto Moses," implies that a long time had elapsed between the death of Moses, and the penning of this chapter of Deuteronomy.

Now in regard to these anachronisms: if it were contended that a Book with these statements in it had been printed and published in the time of Moses, I think that these anachronisms would be CONCLUSIVE EVIdence against such a statement. But we have to consider that the writings of Moses, in whatever state they were left by him, passed through the hands of the guardians of the sacred writings during a period of between eight and nine hundred years to the time of Ezra; that several times of special literary activity occurred within this period, as those of Samuel and the schools of the Prophets, those of David and Solomon and their contemporary Prophets, those of Hezekiah and his copyists (Prov. xxv. 1), and those of Ezra the Scribe (Ezra vii. 6), and that it is inevitable that verbal alterations and additions should have been made in the course of these ages to adapt them to the wants of the people. We shall be strengthened in our sense of the probability of such changes by observing how the feeling of *authorship* is wanting with regard to the Scriptures. The writers themselves, and the custodians of their writings, seem to have had nothing either of the self-importance of *authors*, or any sense of authorship as an ingredient in the authority of the books of which they had the custody. To give and to preserve a clear and authentic account of the history of Israel and God's dealings with His people; to make the sacred records intelligible to the people, and to add any such information as tended to throw light upon the books which they had the care of, seem to have been their main purpose. *We*, in editing an ancient book, add as footnotes any such information or illustrations as may seem necessary. *They* incorporated them in the text. They did this in perfect good faith. The vast majority of the books transcribed by them had no author's name attached. Even the Pentateuch does not claim to have been written by Moses as a whole. Of the authorship of Joshua, Judges, Ruth, the Books of Samuel and Kings, we know absolutely nothing. Moreover, the keepers of the Scriptures had divine authority to teach as Priests or Prophets or both. And hence we cannot be surprised that in handing down to us the ancient records of their nation, they made such additions or alterations in them as made them more intelligible. Take for example the list of the Edomitish Kings in Gen. xxxvi. The original writer had given Esau's genealogy down to the time when he was writing. This appendix to that genealogy completed the history of the Edomitish families, and was added accordingly to the later revision.

It may be worth while to add that this method of dealing with historical documents receives a remarkable illustration from the Book of Ezra. In the second chapter of that book, where the history is dealing with the reign of Cyrus, and about the year B.C. 536, there is inserted a document belonging to the reign of Artaxerxes, and to about the year B.C. 445 (i.e. ninety years later) in which mention is made at v. 63 of the Tirshatha Nehemiah, who did not come to Jerusalem till the later date. And again in Ezra iv. 6, 7 and following verses, where the history is still dealing with the times of Cyrus (about B.C. 536), mention is made by way of illustration of what happened in the time of Xerxes and Artaxerxes, Cyrus's successors, down to about the year B.C. 457, and then the history goes back to the time of Cyrus. But it is not till Ezra vii. that Ezra's own history begins. So again in the Book of Nehemiah, a considerable portion is written by Nehemiah himself, but other parts are the work of some unknown writer, either Ezra or one of his companions. Neh. i.–vii. 6 is written in the first person, and this is resumed again at xiii. 6, to the end of the book. The intermediate chapters are by another hand.

It seems therefore highly probable that the keepers and editors of the Scriptures should have dealt in the same manner with the older books which passed through their hands. It is a further confirmation of this explanation of the introduction of anachronistic passages in the Pentateuch, that the removal of them leaves the context quite unaffected. The genealogy, e. g. of the Edomitish Kings, and of the Dukes of Edom, can be put in or left out, cf. Gen. xxxvi., without any effect upon what goes before or follows after. So, too, the substitution of the modern for the ancient names of cities, disturbs nothing but the single name itself. The same observation applies to those curious antiquarian glosses which recur frequently in the Book of Deuteronomy, and which are generally felt to be scarcely suitable to the person of Moses, or the occasions on which they appear. See Deut. ii. 10–12 ; 20–23 ; iii. 9, 11, 14. In every case they can be left out without affecting the context, a strong indication that they were inserted after the context was written. I think we may conclude that the anachronisms of the Pentateuch are no serious objections to its belonging to the age of Moses.

III. The next objection brought by the "Higher Criticism" against the authenticity of the Pentateuch is that the Hebrew is not the Hebrew of the age of Moses, but that of the later Jewish monarchy; and also that many words and phrases betray the fact that the people had long been settled in Canaan when such passages were written. Among the words and phrases thus objected to, the following may be particularised.

(*a*) In Deut. i. 1, 5; iii. 8; iv. 46 we have the phrase "beyond Jordan[1]" (R.V.) to describe the country on the east of Jordan. Also in the same sense, Num. xxii. 1; xxxii. 32; xxxv. 14, and elsewhere in the later books; and it is argued that the use of the phrase implies that the persons so using it had long been living on the west of Jordan, i.e. in Canaan. If the application of the phrase was uniform, and in every case was used by persons on the west of Jordan to describe the country east of Jordan, there would be considerable force in the argument. But this is by no means the case. In Gen. iv. 10, 11; Deut. iii. 20, 25; Josh. ix. 1, and elsewhere, it means the country west of the Jordan, "the other side" varying in meaning according to the side on which the person speaking is. In Num. xxxii. 19 we find the phrase used in the same breath of both sides: when the Reubenites and Gadites say, "We will not inherit with them on *yonder side* Jordan, ... because our inheritance is fallen unto us on *this side* Jordan, eastward," where the Hebrew

---

[1] Heb. בְּעֵבֶר הַיַּרְדֵּן. The A.V. has "on this side Jordan."

word for *yonder side* and for *this side* is the same. But in other cases the phrase has been fixed to mean the country east of Jordan, irrespective of the position of the speaker, as appears by the name of the country Perea, literally, the *land beyond*, i.e. *to the east* of Jordan, and as in the analogous cases, Gallia trans-alpina, or cis-alpina, or the part of Rome called Transteverina.

(*b*) Objection is again taken to the expression, Deut. xix. 14, "Thou shalt not remove thy neighbour's landmark which they of old times have set in thine inheritance," as if it indicated a long settlement in the land at the time the precept was given; and Deut. v. 14, and Exod. xx. 10, "The stranger that is within thy gates," as being inapplicable to the tents in which they lived in the wilderness. But obviously the law looked forward to the time of their occupation of Canaan. So that this objection is pointless.

(*c*) Again, it is laid down as an axiom by Wellhausen (p. 91), that "agriculture was learned by the Hebrews from the Canaanites in whose land they settled." And it is in accordance with this axiom that all agricultural words and phrases which are found in the Pentateuch, as well as the Jewish Festivals which are founded (as Wellhausen says) upon the agricultural seasons, are supposed to be clear indications that the passages in which such words are found, and the Festivals which have such an origin, must be posterior to the occupation of Canaan by the Hebrews. As if the Israelites could have dwelt for two hundred years in Egypt, the richest corn country in the world, the land where their fathers came in the days of famine to buy corn, the land which for centuries supplied Rome with bread, the land where agriculture was one of the leading occupations of the people, and have been ignorant of common agricultural words, or unfamiliar with the use of the ox and the ass in the labours of the field!

(*d*) We turn then for a few moments to the more important question of the *language* of the Pentateuch.

It is alleged that the Hebrew language in which the Pentateuch is written is not the Hebrew spoken and written in the time of Moses, but that of the later Jewish monarchy. Just therefore as we should pronounce certainly, apart from all other evidence, that the Authorised Version of the Bible was not written in the fourteenth century because the English is quite different from the English, say, of Wycliff's Bible, so they say the Pentateuch could not be written in the fourteenth century before the Christian era, because the Hebrew is the Hebrew of the seventh or eighth century before Christ. But you can see at once the difference between the two cases. In the case of the English Bible we have Wycliff's Bible before us with which to make the comparison. In the case of the Hebrew Bible we have no other work of the age of Moses with which to compare it. The assertion therefore that the Hebrew of the Pentateuch is not the Hebrew of the age of Moses is one which has to be *proved* before we can give our assent to it.

Let us look at the facts. First of all, what was the real interval of time between Moses and, say, King Josiah when the " Higher Criticism " says Deuteronomy was written? The old chronologists placed the Exodus at about B.C. 1490, as you will see by the dates on the margin of your Bibles, being misled as to the Pharaoh of the Exodus, and by some other chronological data in the Bible itself. But recent discoveries have produced unanimity among Egyptologists that the Pharaoh of the Exodus was Menephthah the 2nd, whose accession took place B.C. 1300, which would bring the Exodus about 200 years later, and would place Moses at about the year 1290. The discovery of the Book of the Law in the Temple is placed by chronologists at B. C. 621 (Driver's Introduction to Old Testament,

p. 232). Therefore the interval between Moses and Josiah is under 700 years. The question, therefore, is whether upon philological grounds language could remain as unchanged for 700 years, as a comparison of Jeremiah and the Book of Deuteronomy, if of the age of Moses, would show the Hebrew to have done. There does not appear to be the slightest improbability in this being the case. Compare the Latin of Plautus with the Latin of Gregory the Great 800 years afterwards[1], or the Greek of Thucydides with that of Procopius 1000 years later; or the Arabic spoken at Mecca which is affirmed by the great Arabic scholar Freytag to be precisely the same language as that of the Koran twelve centuries before; or the two Egyptian Papyri spoken of by Brugsch which, though separated by 1000 years in time, yet are of the same stamp and show not the slightest change in grammar, and you will see that there is not the slightest improbability in the Hebrew of the Pentateuch being really the Hebrew of the Mosaic age. The same conclusion may be come to by a careful observation of the proper names of persons and places which show how unchanged the language was of which they were compounded. We must remember too how un-

[1] Smith's "Pentateuch."

changing all things are in the East, manners and customs as well as language—how isolated the Israelites were in their social life, and utterly cut off from intermarriages and other social intercourse with other nations; what an influence upon their written and spoken language the Scriptures would be likely to exercise, like as the Authorised Version has upon our own English tongue, and I think you will come with me to the conviction that there is not any reason on philological grounds to believe that the language of the Pentateuch is not the language of the age of Moses.

I do not, however, wish you to understand that there is NO difference between the language of the Pentateuch and that of the later books. Taking the books of the Old Testament, and dividing them into three periods, the Pentateuch, the books presumably written during the Jewish monarchy, and the books about the time of the Exile (i. e. just before, during, and after the Exile), we find three decided varieties of Hebrew style. The central period gives that of the best and purest Hebrew. The Pentateuch has a more limited vocabulary, and certain archaic spellings[1]. The exilic books have a

[1] As הוא for היא, נער for נערה, צחק (whence Isaac), for שחק, &c.

strong admixture of Aramean forms. There are many words in the Pentateuch which occur nowhere else, and there are many words in the books of the two later periods which are not found in the Pentateuch. And these differences are valuable evidences that the books were really written in the times to which they profess to belong.

IV. The next head of objections—the last which we shall consider this evening—need detain us very few minutes. I do not think it would have been possible for any critic to make so frivolous an objection as " that the Pentateuch betrays a much higher state of civilization than could have existed at so early an age," if he *believed the history* which the Pentateuch contains. The conception of Israel as a rude nomad tribe may be inconsistent with such civilization as the Pentateuchal code supposes. But that any one who believes that the Israelites had been settled in Egypt more than two hundred years, and that Moses their leader and lawgiver was " learned in all the wisdom of the Egyptians," should make such an objection is incredible. The truth is that the more we know of ancient Egypt by that wonderful exploration of her ancient monuments and documents which has been so successfully carried on during the last half century, the more deeply are we impressed with the high level of civilization attained by her in that early age of the world's history. In architecture, in sculpture, in music, in agriculture, in government, in war, in navigation, in the luxuries and embellishments of social life, in manufactures, in her elaborate scheme of historical record, her curious hieroglyphic writing, her sepulchral monuments, her complicated religious system, Egypt stands far ahead of all contemporary nations, and was the leader of the civilization of the world. There is very much in the Mosaic institutions which bears a distinct stamp of connection with Egypt, and so adds a striking testimony to the authenticity of the Books of Moses.

And here I close for to-night. I reserve for my next Lecture the consideration of by far the most formidable objection brought by the "Higher Criticism" against the authenticity of the Pentateuch and the truth of the Mosaic Law, and I shall deal with it at some length. As far as we have gone to-night, I have tried to put you in possession of the chief heads of the arguments by which the "Higher Criticism" attacks the authenticity of the Books of Moses, as far as was possible in so short a compass, and to show you how little cause for uneasiness there is as to the ultimate issue of the conflict between the Scriptures given by God for the guidance of His people in all ages, and the criticisms of a school which rejects all Divine revelation.

The subject of our next Lecture will be the statement of the "Higher Criticism" that "there is no evidence of the existence of the Mosaic Institutions between the time of the Exodus, when the laws purport to have been given, and the later times of the Jewish monarchy;" and the peremptory refutation of it by clear historical evidence.

LECTURE II.

Theory of the "Higher Criticism" with Regard to the Pentateuch (*continued*).

We come now to the last of the grounds on which the "Higher Criticism" impugns the authenticity of the Pentateuch, and denies its historical character. This is, as stated in my last Lecture under head V., "that there is no evidence of the existence of the Mosaic Institutions, between the time of the Exodus, when the Mosaic laws purport to have been given, and the later times of the Jewish monarchy; and that in point of fact the moveable Tabernacle, the Aaronic Priesthood, the Levitical order, and the one place of sacrifice, are all late inventions, with which Moses had nothing whatever to do, and which were unknown till many centuries after his death."

Now I consider this as by far the most plausible ground of the allegations of the "Higher Criticism;" *first* because it professes to rest upon facts, not on the mere fancies of the critics as to what Moses ought to have done, and what the course of history ought to have been; and *secondly* because at first sight the alleged facts seem to have a measure of truth in them. I had for many years in the course of my study of the Old Testament been somewhat puzzled by the absence of more prominent notice of the Mosaic Institutions in the historical books; and less than two years ago in a paper which I printed for private circulation I said that a careful statement of all that we know concerning the existence of the Books of the law between Moses and Ezra ... a collection of references to the law of Moses in the historical books ... or elsewhere ... would help to make a strong case against the conclusions of the "Higher Criticism." But I had never carefully examined the intervening Books of the Old Testament to see whether it really is true that there is no evidence of the existence of the law of Moses between the time of the Exodus and the later Jewish monarchy. Only I felt as I am sure you will all feel with me, that if it really is true that through a period of not less than seven hundred years there was a complete silence in Scripture concerning the Mosaic Institutions it would be a fact difficult to account for, if all the time the law of Moses had been in existence. Hence the importance of our present investigation.

I would further premise that it is also supremely important that all our witnesses should be unimpeachable. It is an essential part of the contention of the "Higher critics" that the Books of Chronicles, which bear such distinct witness to the Mosaic Institutions, are not historical and that their evidence goes for nothing. While, therefore, I hope to show in our latter lectures that they are trustworthy, and that their evidence is conclusive, I shall in the first instance rest the strength of our case upon the other historical books, keeping the Chronicles quite in the background.

My method this evening will be *first* to lay before you three or four of the most prominent Institutions of the Mosaic law as they are contained in the Pentateuch. Then, *secondly*, to adduce some of the statements of the "Higher critics" concerning them. And, *thirdly*, to confront these with passages from the historical Books of the Old Testament from Joshua to Ezra and Nehemiah, and leave you to form your own conclusions.

First, let us take (1) the earliest, and in some points of view one of the most prominent of the Mosaic Institutions, I mean that of the Passover. In Exod. xii. we have the striking account of its institution by Divine command on the eve of the deliverance of Israel from their Egyptian bondage; that great crisis of their national life, celebrated in all after ages by Prophets and Psalmists as the most signal display of God's mercy to His chosen people, the most glorious manifestation of Jehovah's almighty power. And in truth nothing can exceed the grandeur of the occasion, or the significance of the memorial destined to preserve the recollection of it through all ages. The pride of the greatest potentate in the world broken down before the death of all the firstborn of his kingdom: a whole nation, with a wonderful future before them, just poising their wings for their flight into liberty and glory, like a bird let loose from the snare of the fowler —their extraordinary attitude by night, eating the paschal lamb to whose blood, sprinkled upon their houses, they owed their life, eating their unleavened bread in haste with their loins ready girded for the march, their staff in their hand, and their shoes on their feet, waiting for the signal to be off and to be gone. Mark too the other features of the institution. The month in which this happened was thenceforth to be the first month of their year. The day on which it happened was to be kept as a feast to the Lord throughout their generations—" Ye shall keep it as a feast by an ordinance for ever." And as if this was not enough to ensure the perpetual observance of the Passover, it is added (v. 24), "Ye shall observe this thing for an ordinance to thee and to thy sons for ever ... and it shall come to pass when your children shall say unto you What mean ye by this service, that ye shall say, It is the sacrifice of the Lord's Passover, who passed over the houses of the children of Israel in Egypt, when He smote the Egyptians, and delivered our houses—and the people bowed the head and worshipped." The order to keep the Passover is repeated again in Levit. xxiii. 5, and Num. xxviii. 16 and ix. 1–5. And once more in Deut. xvi. 1–8 the commandment is given at some length, "Observe the month Abib, and keep the Passover unto the Lord thy God, for in the month Abib the Lord thy God brought thee out of Egypt by night:" and the limitation is added that the Passover was to be kept only at the place "which the Lord thy God shall choose to put His name in." I must not forget to add that in the first month of the second year of the Exodus a solemn Passover was kept by the children of Israel in the wilderness of Sinai (Num. ix. 1–5) and that this was added to the laws about the Passover, that if any one by reason of uncleanness, or absence on a journey, was unable to keep the Passover on the fourteenth day of the first month, he might do so on the fourteenth day of the second month: a provision of which Hezekiah availed himself according to 2 Chron. xxx. 2.

By the side of the ordinance of the Passover we also find that of the two other great feasts, viz. Pentecost and the Feast of Tabernacles. It may suffice to refer for these to Deut. xvi. 16, 'Three times in a year shall all thy males appear before the Lord thy God, in the place which He shall choose; in the feast of unleavened bread (i. e. the Passover) and in the feast of weeks (Pentecost) and in the feast of tabernacles." (See also Exod. xxiii. 14–17, xxxiv. 18–23, Levit. xxiii., Num. xxviii. xxix). We shall have occasion by and bye to refer to these three festivals.

(2) and (3) We will turn next to two other fundamental institutions of the law of Moses. I mean the separation of the tribe of Levi for the service of the Lord, and the Aaronic priesthood, and we will take the latter first because it came first in order of time. We read in Exod. xxviii. 1 the first distinct separation of Aaron and his sons to the priesthood, "Take unto thee Aaron thy brother, and his sons with him . . . that he may minister unto me in the Priest's office, even Aaron, Nadab and Abihu,

Eleazar and Ithamar, Aaron's sons "—where you have Aaron the High Priest, and his sons as assistant Priests. In the following chapters we have an elaborate account of the garments to be worn by Aaron and his sons respectively, of the sacrifices to be offered at their consecration, of the anointing oil with which Aaron was to be anointed, and among other things of the Urim and Thummim by means of which the High Priest should enquire of the Lord on matters of high religious or national concern. There are also many precise laws as to the portions of the sacrifices belonging to the Priests, and as to the various functions exclusively belonging to Aaron and to his sons. You will all doubtless remember especially the imposing ceremony of the High Priest entering once a year within the vail, with the blood of the sacrifice and the sweet incense, and confession of sins over the scapegoat that was to be sent into the wilderness. And then to show the perpetuity of the office, and its continuance in the family of Aaron, it is enacted in Exod. xxix. 29 that the holy garments of Aaron shall be his son's after him. And accordingly when the time came that Aaron must die, the Lord bid Moses take Aaron and his son Eleazar up into Mount Hor, and there strip Aaron of his priestly garments and put them upon Eleazar his son, and Moses did so. And thenceforth Eleazar appears as the High Priest, as e. g. in the second numbering of the people (Num. xxvi. 63), in the decision about the daughters of Zelophehad (Num. xxvii. 2), and other occasions, but especially in connection with one very important event, the appointment of Joshua to be the successor of Moses as the lay chief of the congregation. We read as follows in Num. xxvii. 18, "And the Lord said unto Moses, Take thee Joshua the son of Nun . . . and set him before Eleazar the Priest, and before all the congregation, and give him a charge in their sight . . . And he shall stand before Eleazar the Priest, who shall ask counsel for him after the judgment of Urim before the Lord," and so on: I call your special attention to this peculiar function of the High Priest in relation to the civil rulers—enquiring of God for him through the Urim and Thummim of the priestly ephod— because I shall have to refer to it by and bye. The High Priesthood of Eleazar seems to have lasted through the book of Joshua, his death being recorded in the last verse of that book. It may however be doubted whether he was not already dead at the time of the events recorded in Josh. xxii. seeing that at v. 30 his son is called simply "Phinehas the Priest," and that the other designation of him "Phinehas the son of Eleazar the Priest" is equally compatible with his being the High Priest at this time. But this by the way. Anyhow we know from Judg. xx. 28 that Phinehas succeeded his father Eleazar.

But this provision for a perpetual supply of Priests of the House of Aaron did not exhaust the provision made by the law of Moses for the service of God. The whole of the remaining families of the tribe of Levi were separated to assist the Priests in their ministrations. In Num. ii. 5 ff. we read that the Lord spake unto Moses, saying, "Bring the tribe of Levi near, and present them before Aaron the Priest that they may minister unto him. And they shall ... do the service of the Tabernacle. And thou shalt give the Levites unto Aaron and his sons; they are wholly given unto him out of the children of Israel." And it is further explained (v. 13) that the Levites were thus taken into the service of the Tabernacle in exchange for the first-born who had been hallowed unto the Lord on the Passover night when the first-born of Egypt were smitten. The consequence of this was that the tribe of Levi was not numbered when the other tribes were, as we read in Num. i. And that when the land of Canaan was divided among the twelve tribes of Israel, the tribe of Levi received no inheritance, "the Lord was their inheritance," as it is said more than once; that is to say, that instead of having land like the other tribes they were to be wholly maintained by their allotted portion of the tithes, and of the beasts offered in sacrifice by their brethren of the other tribes.

As the result of this whole legislation, as appears equally from Exodus, Leviticus, Numbers and Deuteronomy—except that I do not think there is any direct mention in Deuteronomy of the High Priest—the Israelitish people as a fundamental part of their constitution had a hierarchy drawn exclusively from one of their tribes. It consisted of an hereditary High Priest, a person of the highest dignity and importance in the community, his assistant Priests, and a large body of inferior ministers scattered over the whole country. The whole external religion of the community, which by the same legislative code was of a most elaborate and conspicuous kind, was under the control and management of this one tribe.

(4) We turn next to another singular and remarkable ordinance of the Mosaic law. The worship of God, with the costly system of sacrifice

and offerings, and the ministration of High Priest, and Priests, and Levites, and all the apparatus of altars, and tables, and candlesticks, and the ark of the covenant, was by the law strictly confined to one place. Again and again it is said, Thou shalt sacrifice, &c., "at the place which the Lord thy God shall choose to place His name there—not in any of thy gates, ... but at the place which the Lord thy God shall choose to place His name in" (Deut. xvi. 2, 5, 6, 11, 16). "Unto the place which the Lord your God shall choose out of all your tribes to put His name there, even unto His habitation shall ye seek, and thither shalt thou come, and thither ye shall bring your burnt offerings and your sacrifices," and so on (Deut. xii. 5, 11, 14, 18, 21). But these precepts in Deut. apply to the time when they should have crossed over Jordan, and the Lord should have given them rest (Deut. xii. 10). But, meanwhile, while they were still in the wilderness, and still moving from place to place, this unity of altar, and sacrifice, and place of worship, was equally secured by the remarkable provision of the moveable TABERNACLE. The House of God, the place which He chose to put His Name there, was not yet a fixed place on the earth. But still there was only one place at any given time where God's Name was recorded (Exod. xx. 24) and that was wherever the Tabernacle was (see Levit. xvii. 1–9 and elsewhere). The whole history of the Tabernacle in Exod. Levit. Num. and Deut. is most remarkable. The pattern of it showed to Moses in the mount (Exod. xxv. 9–40; xxvi. 30; Acts vii. 44; Heb. viii. 5): the command, "Let them make me a sanctuary that I may dwell among them" (Exod. xxv. 8), followed by the promise, "There will I meet with the children of Israel, and I will sanctify the Tabernacle ... and I will dwell among the children of Israel, and will be their God" (Exod. xxix. 43–45); the elaborate description of its material, structure and furniture (xxv.–xxvii.); the description of the execution of the work by Bezaleel and Aholiab, and then of its solemn rearing on the first day of the first month of the second year, and the taking possession of His sanctuary by the Lord of glory, when "a cloud covered the tent of the congregation, and the glory of the Lord filled the Tabernacle" (Exod. xl. 35), all these are particulars which give an unrivalled importance and dignity to the Tabernacle of the congregation. Nor are the other details concerning it of less solemn interest. The cloud of the Lord resting upon it by day and the fire by night, in the sight of all Israel throughout their journeyings, symbolising God's gracious Presence in the midst of His people; its being taken up when they were to go forward on their journeys, and their resting still so long as the cloud was not taken up from over the Tabernacle (Exod. xl. 34-38); the gathering together of the whole congregation to the door of the Tabernacle on solemn occasions, such as the consecration of Aaron and his sons to the Priesthood (Levit. viii.); the frequent communing of the Lord with Moses "from out of the Tabernacle of the congregation" (Levit. i. 1; Num. xii. 4, 5; xvi. 42, 43); the jealousy with which the sanctity of the Tabernacle was guarded, and the severity with which the profanation of it was punished (Levit. x. 1-3; xv. 31); the provision for the place of the Tabernacle in the camp, for the encampment. of the Levites immediately around it, for the offices of the Priests and Levites respectively in the carriage of it and of the vessels pertaining to it (Num. i. 50-53; iii. 23 ff.; iv.), and, not to particularise further, such solemn scenes as that described in Deut. xxxi. 14, 15, when Moses and Joshua were summoned to the Tabernacle that Joshua might receive his charge as successor to Moses, and the Lord appeared in the Tabernacle in a pillar of a cloud, and the pillar of the cloud stood over the door of the Tabernacle—I say all this throws a halo of sanctity and dignity around the Tabernacle of the congregation which places it in the forefront of the institutions of the law of Moses, and, may I not add, gives it a very high place in the reverential affection of all the servants of God. But we shall not have a complete view of the Tabernacle of the congregation, or tent of meeting, unless we add that in it was kept "the ark of the covenant." These two were inseparable, and wherever one was we may infer the presence of the other. · The ark (Exod. xxv. 10-22) was a chest of acacia wood, overlaid with pure gold within and without, about 3 ft. 9 in. in length, and 2 ft. 3 in. in breadth and in height. In it were placed the two tables of stone, on which were engraved the words of the covenant, even the ten commandments (Exod. xxxiv. 28 ; Deut. iv. 13 ; x. 4), which formed the basis of the Covenant between God and the children of Israel. On this ark rested the mercy-seat, and over the mercy-seat were the two cherubims of gold, whose wings stretched from end to end of the mercy-seat. And there it was that God " who dwelleth between the cherubims" promised to meet with Moses and commune with him of all things which He had to give in command-

ment to the children of Israel (Exod. xxv. 22).
You see the ark was as it were the very kernel
of the Tabernacle, its chief treasure; it was "the
ark of God's strength," the seat of His Presence
and His Power.

The above then were a few of the most conspicuous and characteristic features of the Mosaic Law.

SECONDLY. The "Higher Criticism" tells us that in these grand and elevating narratives, in these holy institutions by which the hearts of thousands have been made to feel the nearness and the awful holiness of God, there is not one word of historical truth. To use Professor Kuenen's phrase, they are "fictitious narratives." The narratives which pretend to be contemporary with Moses and to give an account of the ordaining of these institutions by the direct command of God, are really the inventions of an age many hundred years—7 or 800—later than Moses, and have their origin not in any revelation, but in the political needs of the heads of the Jewish community, in an age shortly before, during, or after, the Babylonish captivity. The Book of Deuteronomy, we are told, was composed in the reign of King Josiah, when Hilkiah the High Priest pretended that during the repairs of the Temple he had found "the Book of the

Law"—i. e. the Book of Deuteronomy, in the Temple, in the place where, according to Deut. xxxi. 24, it was ordered to be kept by the side of the ark (2 Kings xxii. 8). Shaphan the scribe, Josiah the king, Huldah the prophetess, and all the elders and people of Israel believed that the book found was the veritable work of Moses. But unluckily there was no "higher critic" at Jerusalem to expose the imposture. Had they had the advantage of having Professor Kuenen among them he would have told them that this book which they thought was 700 or 800 years old, had quite recently been written [1] and placed there for the express purpose of being found, and frightening them into a reformation (Kuenen, Hexateuch, p. 215). The same opinion as to the age of Deuteronomy is expressed by Wellhausen, who tells us that "It is in evidence that Deuteronomy became known in the year B.C. 621, and that it was *unknown* up to that date" (p. 408). He tells us (p. 402) that as this book is called in 2 Kings "the book of the Torah" (i. e. the *law*), "it was the first, and in its time the only book of its kind" (p. 402). In like manner (p. 408) "It is in evidence that the remaining Torah of the Pentateuch

---

[1] In the reign of Manasseh (Driver, p. 82), others say Hezekiah.

became known in the year B.C. 444 and was unknown until then." And he adds, "This shows in the first place and puts it beyond question, that Deuteronomy is the first, and the priestly Torah the second stage of the legislation. But in the second place, as we are accustomed to infer the date of the composition of Deuteronomy from its publication and introduction by Josiah, so we must infer the date of the composition of the priestly code (i.e. the rest of the Pentateuch) from its publication and introduction by Ezra and Nehemiah" (p. 408). Kuenen also says (p. 192), "We are fully justified in concluding: (1) that Deuteronomy was not known before the last quarter of the seventh century B.C., and (2) that the priestly laws and narratives were still in the nascent stage in Ezekiel's time (592–570 B.C.), and did not exist in the form in which we have them in the Hexateuch before the time of Ezra and Nehemiah."

I think then, that without any further extracts from the chief writers of the "Higher Criticism," I may now say, without any fear of misrepresenting them, that they lay it down as an ascertained truth that the law of Moses, the Torah, did not exist in the times between Moses and the Babylonish captivity. That the first instalment of it came to light in the reign of

Josiah and the second in the time of Artaxerxes the King of Persia, under the auspices of Ezra and Nehemiah. I ought to add that it is a further development of their theory that continual additions were made to the priestly code, i.e. to Exodus, Leviticus, and Numbers, for fully 100 years later before the Pentateuch finally received its present form. Their strongest argument, as I have said, in favour of this conclusion, is that *there is no evidence of the existence of the Mosaic institutions between the time of the Exodus and the later times of the Jewish monarchy;* and if this was really true it would be a very weighty argument against the authority of the Pentateuch.

I proceed therefore now, THIRDLY, to lay before you such passages as I have found in the historical books between the Pentateuch and Ezra and Nehemiah, as refer plainly to those leading characteristic institutions of the Mosaic law, the Passover, the hereditary Priesthood, the Levites, and the Tabernacle, and will then ask you to form your own conclusions as to the truth or falsehood of the "Higher Criticism."

I would observe *in limine* that one single clear example of the existence of any one of these four characteristic Mosaic institutions in the time we are dealing with would be very strong evidence of the existence of the law which prescribed it. But that the combination of examples of the co-existence of all four is a threefold cord which cannot be broken. I would observe also that in all such cases incidental notices are the strongest kind of evidence, because they are like undesigned coincidences. They can only arise because they are true, and they have this further effect: they silence the argument which might be drawn from the absence of more notices, by showing that the writers would not have given us even the notices which they have if incidental circumstances had not led them to do so.

With these preliminary remarks we will now proceed (1) to see how the case stands with regard to the Passover, and the other two feasts of weeks and of Tabernacles.

We have already seen that according to Num. ix. 1–5 the second Passover was celebrated in the wilderness of Sinai, in the first month of the second year after they were come up out of the land of Egypt. We pass on to the Book of Joshua, and there we read, at ch. v. 10, "And the children of Israel encamped in Gilgal, and kept the Passover on the fourteenth day of the month" ("the first month," we learn from Josh. iv. 19). That was the *third* recorded Passover.

The *fourth* recorded Passover took place in the reign of Hezekiah. The writer of the book of Kings does not mention it though he dwells generally upon Hezekiah's piety and zeal, and the faithfulness with which "he followed the Lord, and kept his commandments which the Lord commanded Moses" (see, too, 2 Kings xviii. 12). But in 2 Chron. xxx. we have a full account of Hezekiah's Passover, with the remarkable circumstance that it was kept in the second month, according to the provision of Num. ix., and that some of the tribes of Asher, Manasseh, Zebulun, and Ephraim, took part in it. It was done, the writer adds, according to the law of Moses the man of God (v. 16).

The *fifth* recorded Passover is that held in the reign of Josiah, as related in 2 Kings xxiii. and in 2 Chron. xxxv. Of this Passover the first writer tells us that the king issued a command, saying, "Keep the Passover unto the Lord your God, as it is written in the Book of this covenant" (i.e. the lately discovered Deuteronomy). And he goes on to say, "Surely there was not holden such a Passover from the days of the Judges that judged Israel, nor in all the days of the Kings of Israel, nor of the Kings of Judah. But in the eighteenth year of King Josiah wherein this Passover was holden to the

Lord in Jerusalem." He adds that "there was no king like Josiah that turned to the Lord with all his might according to all the law of Moses" (v. 25). In like manner the writer of 2 Chron. xxxv. tells us that "Josiah kept a Passover unto the Lord in Jerusalem: and they killed the Passover on the fourteenth day of the first month." And he goes on to say how everything was done according to the word of the Lord by the hand of Moses, and then adds "there was no Passover like to that kept in Israel from the days of Samuel the Prophet. Neither did all the kings keep such a Passover as Josiah kept" (v. 18).

The *sixth* recorded Passover is that kept by the Jews who were returned from Babylon in the sixth year of the reign of Darius, King of Persia, under the government of Zerubbabel, and the High Priesthood of Joshua, and under the influence of the Prophets Haggai and Zechariah, some sixty or seventy years before Ezra and Nehemiah came up from Babylon. It was immediately after the rebuilding of the Temple was completed, and the celebration is thus described: "And the children of the captivity kept the Passover upon the fourteenth day of the first month.... And the children of Israel which were come again out of captivity, and all such as had separated themselves unto them from the filthiness of the land to seek the Lord God of Israel, did eat, and kept the feast of unleavened bread seven days with joy" (Ezra vi. 19–22): where I would observe how naturally the Passover, and the unleavened bread, and the cleanness of the partakers, are mentioned as things well-known to all, and parts of their ancient national customs to which they gladly return.

I will also ask you to notice that besides these *six* recorded Passovers we have hints of others not recorded in the two passages in 2 Kings and 2 Chron. The writer of 2 Kings xxiii. 22 says, "surely there was not holden such a Passover (as that in the eighteenth year of King Josiah) from the days of the Judges that judged Israel, nor in all the days of the Kings of Israel and Judah." And the writer of 2 Chron. says of the same Passover, "there was no Passover like to that kept in Israel from the days of Samuel the Prophet, neither did all the Kings of Israel keep such a Passover as Josiah kept" (v. 18). Surely this implies that other Passovers were kept of which we have no special record. Of one such unrecorded Passover we have an unmistakeable hint in 1 Kings ix. 25, where we are told that "Three times in a year did Solomon offer burnt offerings and peace offerings upon the altar which he had built, ... and he burnt incense upon the altar which was before the Lord." What can these *three times in a year* possibly be but the three great festivals at which the Israelites were to appear before the Lord at the place which the Lord should choose to place His Name there, of which the Passover was one. And so accordingly the chronicler tells us that Solomon offered these offerings "according to the commandment of Moses, three times in the year, even in the feast of unleavened bread, and in the feast of weeks, and in the feast of Tabernacles" (2 Chron. viii. 13). In harmony with this we read in 1 Kings viii. 2 that "all the men of Israel assembled themselves unto King Solomon at the feast in the month Ethanim which is the seventh month," of which a fuller account is given in 2 Chron. vii. where it is added among other things that "Solomon kept the feast seven days" (v. 8); and that "on the three-and-twentieth day of the seventh month, he sent the people away into their tents" (v. 10). A comparison with Levit. xxiii. 34 will show beyond any possible doubt that the feast of Tabernacles was the feast meant. This feast of Tabernacles was also kept by the Jews who had returned from Babylon in the time of Zerubbabel (Ezra iii. 4), still, be it well remembered, some seventy years or more before Ezra came from Babylon. See, too, Zech. xiv. 16-19. And now I would make the remark which the comparative paucity of recorded observances of the Passover suggests, viz. that we must be extremely cautious in drawing conclusions from the silence of Scripture on any particular subject. The Scriptures do not give us an exhaustive account of the whole times of which they treat, nor of all the events which happened in those times, but only such a selection as seemed good to the Wisdom of God. For example, thirty-eight years of the forty passed in the wilderness have absolutely no events assigned to them. They are a blank. The first thirty years or so of Saul's reign are passed over in almost complete silence. The long reign of Uzziah—fifty-two years—occupies four verses in 2 Kings. Even then if we had not had the distinct record of six celebrations of the Passover, and those hints of others contained in 1 Kings ix. 25, and 2 Kings xxiii. 22; 2 Chron. viii. 13, and xxxv. 18, it would have been a very precarious conclusion from the silence of Scripture that no celebration of the Passover had taken place. And notice further how the justice of this observation is borne out by the fact that all the records we have arise from incidental circumstances. Joshua's Passover was the *first* celebrated in Canaan. Hezekiah's was part of a great reformation coming after the wicked reign of King Ahaz, when the Temple had been shut, and the sacrifices had not been offered up, and the lamps had been put out, and idolatrous practices introduced into the Temple itself. Josiah's was in like manner part of a similar reformation coming after the long reign of the idolatrous Manasseh, and stimulated by the discovery of the Book of Deuteronomy in the Temple. The Passover, recorded Ezra vi., was a great event, being the first after the return of the Jews from Babylon. Solomon's Passover and two other festivals are mentioned merely in connection with the altar which he had just built unto the Lord; and the celebration of the Feast of Tabernacles in connection with the great event of bringing the ark of the Lord to its new place in the Temple which was just completed. Had it not been for these remarkable incidents the ordinary history might well have run its course without any mention whatever of the celebration of these festivals.

However, the result is that we have direct, clear, and certain evidence, that as far as the celebration of the three great festivals ordained by Moses goes, the law of Moses was known and put in practice between the time of the Exodus, and the coming of Ezra and Nehemiah from Babylon to Jerusalem.

(2) and (3) We turn then next to the Hereditary Priesthood of Aaron, and the separation of the rest of the tribe of Levi to be assistants to their co-tribesmen the Priests. Are there any traces of the existence of these institutions in the times between the Exodus and Ezra? We have seen the transfer of the High Priesthood from Aaron to his son Eleazar, and how Eleazar was "the Priest" while Joshua was the civil leader of Israel. From a passage in the Book of Judges xx. 28, we learn that, at the time of the great civil war with the tribe of Benjamin, Phinehas, the famous son of Eleazar, the son of Aaron, stood before the ark of the covenant as High Priest, and performed that remarkable function which was the prerogative of the High Priest to "enquire of the Lord" at the instigation of the civil ruler. So that you not only have in this incidental notice the proof that Phinehas succeeded his father Eleazar in the priesthood, but have also a distinct reference to the institution of Urim and Thummim described in Exod. xxviii. 30; Levit. viii. 8;

Num. xxvii. 21, as well as to "the ark of the Covenant."

Passing down the stream of time a hundred years, or more, to 1 Sam. i. we find Eli the High Priest, with his two sons, Hophni and Phinehas, the acting Priests under him. We learn that he resided at Shiloh where we know that the Tabernacle, or House of God, was (Judg. xviii. 31; Josh. xviii. 1; Ps. lxxviii. 60; and Jer. vii. 12), at which Aaron, Eleazar, and Phinehas had ministered before the Lord, and where the ark of God was, "the ark of the covenant of the Lord of Hosts, which dwelleth between the cherubims" (iv. 4), and where pious Israelites went up year by year to worship, and to sacrifice to the Lord of Hosts. We know too that Eli was the descendant of Aaron the High Priest, because the message of God to him by the Prophet, who was sent to rebuke him for the iniquity of his sons, was, "Did I plainly appear unto the house of thy father when they were in Egypt ... and did I choose him out of all the tribes of Israel to be my Priest, to offer upon mine altar, to burn incense, and to wear an ephod before me?" and so on. We know too that he was succeeded in the High Priesthood by his descendants down to about the fourth generation, as we shall see by and bye. Once more we know incidentally from 1 Chron. xxiv. 3, that Ahimelech the great grandson of Eli was of the house of Ithamar the son of Aaron. Putting all this together it becomes absolutely certain, if we believe our authorities, that *Eli was the hereditary High Priest of the House of Aaron.* Only we do not know why or how it was that the High Priesthood passed away from the line of Eleazar, to the line of his brother Ithamar; nor who succeeded Phinehas, the last High Priest we know of of the line of Eleazar till Zadok in the time of David. Nor does it matter. But I have been led to enter into these particulars because of the extraordinary statements of Wellhausen who, in bold defiance of all historical documents, denies the Aaronic Priesthood, denies the High Priesthood of Eli, makes him merely the Priest of a great sanctuary belonging to the tribe of Ephraim at Shiloh, denies all connection with Aaron to Zadok, who, he says, was made a Priest by David, and tells us that "the suddenness with which the full-grown hierocracy descended on the wilderness from the skies is only matched by the suddenness with which it disappeared in Canaan leaving *no trace behind it*" (p. 127).

Passing on, perhaps some forty or fifty years later, to the reign of Saul, we light on a description of one of his conflicts with the Philistines, and at 1 Sam. xiv. 3, we are told that among those that accompanied Saul was "Ahiah, the son of Ahitub, Ichabod's brother, the son of Phinehas, the son of Eli, the Lord's Priest in Shiloh, wearing an ephod." And at v. 18 we read that "Saul said unto Ahiah, Bring hither the ark of God:" or rather as it is in the Septuagint and the phrase requires "*the ephod*" mentioned in v. 3, for the purpose of enquiring of the Lord by Urim and Thummim, in accordance with Num. xxvii. 21. I venture to think that here again we have in Canaan "*some trace of the full-grown Hierarchy which descended on the wilderness from the skies.*"

We pass on yet a few years, perhaps ten or thereabouts, and we light on the incident of David's flight from the persecution of Saul. We read in 1 Sam. xxi. that after his touching parting with Jonathan he came to Nob to Ahimelech the Priest, and in the course of this and the following chapter we learn that Ahimelech (who was either the same person as Ahijah, or his brother) was the High Priest, that he was the son of Ahitub, the son of Phinehas, the son of Eli; that the tabernacle was then at Nob, the city of the Priests, and that Ahimelech dwelt there at the head of eighty-five Priests, all of his father's house; that he had the ephod with which to enquire of the Lord, and that the table with the shew-bread was there in accordance with Exod. xxv. 30; Levit. xxiv. 5, 6; and we learn that he was the father of Abiathar who was High Priest all through the reign of David. Here again then we have "some trace" of "the hierocracy which descended from the skies."

I need but just glance at the next "trace" in 1 Sam. xxii. 20, and xxiii. 1–12, where we read that when Saul slaughtered Ahimelech and the eighty-five " Priests of the Lord," one of Ahimelech's sons, Abiathar, escaped and took "an ephod in his hand," and came to David to Keilah. Hence David was able to "enquire of the Lord," as we read in v. 9, " David said to Abiathar the Priest, Bring hither the ephod," and then follows the enquiry, and the Lord's answers, and so again 1 Sam. xxx. 7. I refer you once more to Num. xxvii. 21. This Abiathar continued with David through his whole reign as "Priest" in conjunction with Zadok (2 Sam. viii. 17, xx. 25). He was faithful to David in Absalom's rebellion (2 Sam. xv. 35, 36), but was deposed by Solomon for taking part with Adonijah (1 Kings ii. 26, 27).

And here I would repeat the remark, which

I made with reference to the observance of the Passover, that almost all the notices of the High Priests are incidental. Had not the civil war with Benjamin occurred, had not Samuel's birth required especial notice, had not the ark been captured by the Philistines, had not Saul taken Ahijah with him to the Philistine war, had not David fled to Ahimelech, we might never have heard of Phinehas as High Priest, or of Eli or his sons, or Ahitub, or Ahijah, or Ahimelech, and yet there they were fulfilling their office generation after generation in succession to Aaron their ancestor, in exact accordance with the law of Moses. So precarious is the argument from the mere silence of Scripture!

As regards the notices of Priests and Levites in the times between the Exodus and Solomon, it may suffice to refer to the eighty-five Priests at Nob with Ahimelech, to Hophni and Phinehas with Eli (1 Sam. ii.) to the mention of the Levites in 1 Sam. vi. 15 as taking down the ark of the Lord when it returned from the country of the Philistines, corroborating as it does the evidence of 1 Chron. vi. that Obed-edom the Gittite, in whose house the ark rested three months (2 Sam. vi. 11) was a Levite; to the mention in 2 Sam. xv. 24 of "Zadok and all the Levites that were with him bearing the ark of the covenant of

God," the casual mention in Judg. xvii. of the Levite who became Micah's Priest, and afterwards Priest to the tribe of Dan (Judg. xviii. 30), and of the other Levite whose terrible story is told Judg. xix., xx., and in still earlier times to the bearing of the ark across the Jordan by the Priests (Josh. iii. 6, 8, 13, 15, 17; iv. 9, 17), to the non-assignment of land to the Levites (Josh. xiii. 14, 33; xviii. 9), and lastly to the assignment of forty-eight cities to the tribe of Levi, both Priests and Levites, as fully described in Josh. xxi. Unless all these notices are to be arbitrarily blotted out from the page of history, I submit to every candid mind that they too are very distinct traces of the "hierocracy which descended full-blown from Heaven."

(4) We return LASTLY to the "Tabernacle of the congregation" or "Tent of meeting," as the Hebrew is more correctly rendered. Are there any traces of the existence of this Tabernacle in the times between the Exodus and the reign of Solomon? We examine first our earliest authority the Book of Joshua. In xviii. 1 we read this explicit statement, "and the whole congregation of the children of Israel assembled together at Shiloh, and set up the Tabernacle of the congregation there," and again at xix. 51,

we read (after the description of the different inheritances of the seven tribes), " These are the inheritances which Eleazar the Priest, and Joshua the son of Nun, and the heads of the fathers of the tribes of the children of Israel divided for an inheritance by lot in Shiloh, before the Lord, at the door of the Tabernacle of the congregation." And I will ask you particularly to notice the expression " before the Lord," as indicating the Lord's special Presence at the Tabernacle, of which there are such numerous examples in the Pentateuch, and to compare with it Josh. xviii. 6, 8, 10. We pass on to Josh. xxii. where we have the remarkable story about the two and a half tribes who had their inheritance on the east of Jordan. You will remember that Reuben, Gad, and the half-tribe of Manasseh, though they had received their inheritance in Gilead and Bashan, yet accompanied their brothers across the Jordan to assist them in taking possession of Canaan. In this chapter we read that, having fully accomplished their task, Joshua dismissed them with a blessing to return to their inheritance on the east of Jordan. But when they reached the Jordan it occurred to them that in times to come the tribes west of Jordan might perhaps refuse to recognise them as a true portion of God's people Israel, and say to them, "Ye have no part in the Lord." And so their children would become as the heathen. They therefore built a great altar, and called it the altar of witness. But when their brothers, the nine tribes and a half, on the west of Jordan heard of it they thought it was intended to be a schismatical altar, set up in rivalry to the one Altar before the Tabernacle. Accordingly a great national meeting was held at Shiloh, the result of which was that Phinehas, the son of Eleazar, and ten princes, a prince from each tribe, were sent off in hot haste as an embassy to the two and a half tribes to demand an explanation, and to declare war against them if they persisted in maintaining an altar for sacrifice " beside the altar of the Lord our God." In the course of their message " from the whole congregation of Israel," in which it is to be presumed Phinehas was the spokesman, we find this remarkable expression, " Notwithstanding if the land of your possession be unclean, then pass ye over unto the land of the possession of the Lord, wherein the Lord's Tabernacle dwelleth, and take possession among us: but rebel not against the Lord, nor rebel against us, in building you an altar beside the altar of the Lord our God." The explanation of the Reubenites and Gadites was quite satisfactory, and so the matter ended peaceably. In 2 Sam. vii. 6, we find incidentally a few words which cover the whole time we are considering. When David proposed to build a Temple at Jerusalem, he said to Nathan, "See now I dwell in a house of cedar, but the ark of God dwelleth within curtains." But the answer of God was, "Shalt thou build me an House for Me to dwell in? Whereas I have not dwelt in any house since the time that I brought up the children of Israel out of Egypt even to this day, but have walked in a tent and in a Tabernacle." We have a curious identification too of the Tabernacle which still existed in David's time with that set up by Moses, in the incidental circumstance mentioned in 1 Kings i. 39, that "Zadok took an horn of oil out of the Tabernacle, and anointed Solomon." It is clear from Exod. xxxi. 11, xxxix. 38, that the sacred anointing oil was kept in the Tabernacle as part of its furniture. In this connection we have also the testimony of 1 Kings viii. 1–11, that at the solemn dedication of Solomon's Temple at the feast of Tabernacles the Priests and Levites "brought up the ark of the Lord, and the Tabernacle of the congregation, and all the holy vessels that were in the Tabernacle," and placed the ark of the covenant, containing the "two tables of stone which Moses put there at Horeb, in the most holy place, even under the wings of the cherubim." The chronicler (2 Chr. i. 3) adds expressly that it was "the Tabernacle of the congregation of God which Moses, the servant of the Lord, had made in the wilderness." But we must not listen to the chronicler just yet. And now with these testimonies fresh in your minds, let your thoughts run back to those scenes and places which we were thinking of a few minutes ago, the place in Shiloh where Eli and his sons sacrificed and ministered to the Lord, where the ark of God was, where the lamp was lit every night by the young Levite Samuel; or to the place at Nob where Ahimelech and his eighty-five assistant Priests were in attendance, where the table of shew-bread was, and the ephod, and Goliath's sword,—is it possible to nurture the smallest doubt in your minds that that place called in 1 Sam. "the House of the Lord," and "the Temple of the Lord" was none other than the TABERNACLE of the congregation, which was pitched in the wilderness by Moses, and which was brought up to Jerusalem by Solomon? And then there is the further testimony of the Prophet Jeremiah that the Tabernacle was for a long time at Shiloh. He was rebuking the foolish confidence of the Jews in his day who thought that because the Temple of the Lord was at Jerusalem no harm could happen to them though they continued in their sins (Jer. vii. 2–11), and then he goes on at verse 12, "But go ye now unto my place which was in Shiloh, where I set my name at the first, and see what I did to it for the wickedness of my people Israel, . . ." and adds, "I will do unto this House as I have done to Shiloh." And once more, xxvi. 6, standing in the courts of the Temple at Jerusalem, he said to the people, "Thus saith the Lord, I will make this house like Shiloh." We may add the passage in Judg. xix. 31, which tells us that Micah's graven image remained at Dan "all the time that the House of God was in Shiloh."

But even this does not exhaust the evidence. Professor Stanley Leathes, in his lately published work "The Law in the Prophets," has shown that all the Prophets, those of Israel as well as those of Judah, the earliest as well as the later ones, were intimately acquainted with the Pentateuch, and the old books of Scripture. Their writings are full of references to the creation, the deluge, the destruction of Sodom and Gomorrha, the history of the Patriarchs, the destruction of the Amorites, the deliverance from

Egypt, and other events recorded in the Pentateuch, besides innumerable words and phrases unquestionably borrowed from or referring to it. But for details I refer you to the book itself.

And now with reference to the great question which has been occupying us through this and part of the preceding Lecture, whether there is any evidence of the existence of the Mosaic institutions between the times of the Exodus, and the later times of the Jewish monarchy, and whether there is a shred of truth in the assertion of the "Higher Criticism" that the Mosaic institutions, including the great Feasts, the moveable Tabernacle with its furniture, the Aaronic Priesthood and the Levitical Order, and the one altar of sacrifice, were all late inventions seven or eight hundred years after Moses. I would put it to every honest mind, if the Pentateuch did not exist, why were the Passover and the Feast of Tabernacles kept, as we have seen they were? Why was there an unbroken succession of High Priests from Aaron to Abiathar and Zadok, as we have seen there was, and onwards down to the destruction of Jerusalem? Why was there a body of Priests and Levites always turning up as occasion required them? Why through the most unsettled times was there one Tabernacle with the ark of the Covenant, the table of shew-bread, the ephod with which the High Priest enquired of the Lord at the instigation of the civil ruler, and the lamp kept burning by night; whither men came to worship and offer sacrifice, and where the High Priest and his assistants always abode? Till I can get some better answer to these questions than that with which Kuenen disposes of the narrative of the Altar of witness, "It is an absolutely unhistorical invention, framed to defend the doctrine of a unique sanctuary" (p. 109), I shall adhere to the ancient belief which has come down to us with the sanction of 3000 years; the belief which accounts for all these things in the simplest and most natural way; the belief that the law of Moses in all its essential features did exist and was operative through all those dark ages; the belief, let me add, that those Holy Scriptures to which our risen Lord referred, "the law of Moses, the Prophets, and the Psalms," will hold their place of supreme authority and loving credence in the Church of God, when the speculations of a presumptuous and sceptical criticism shall have long been laid to rest in an unhallowed and dishonoured grave.

LECTURE III.

Miscellaneous Remarks on the Earlier Books of the Old Testament, and their Authenticity.

In my two first Lectures I have endeavoured to show you that the views of the "Higher Criticism," however prevalent at the present day, and whatever encouragement may be given to them by English Divines, are not trustworthy. I have thought that it might be a useful addition to what was then said, if before proceeding to the examination of the Books of Chronicles, I put before you a few miscellaneous considerations with respect to the earlier Books of the Old Testament which may help to give you a right conception of them, and to establish their authenticity.

And First I would ask you to notice the unique character of the Scriptures. The unity of purpose of Almighty God from the Creation to the end of the world is traced in them with astonishing clearness and consistency, as is the history of the development of that purpose in the successive ages of the world. There is nothing like it in the literature of Greece or Rome, or Egypt or Assyria or India, or any other race of men of whom we have any knowledge. Even the most advanced critics, who split up the Pentateuch into countless fragments, are struck with this unity of design. Let us trace it hastily in its great outlines, and in its two great branches,—the purpose of God, and the actual history of the human race [1].

And (1) as regards the purpose of God. The Scriptures begin with an account of the creation of the world, and, as the crowning act, the creation of man in the image of God, and the gift to him of this earth for his abode, with the absolute dominion over every other living creature upon the earth. There was the first step in God's gracious purpose of love and favour to the human race. After the sad episode of the temptation and fall of man, and his consequent loss of the happy and peaceful abode provided for him in the days of primeval innocence, this same purpose of love takes the direction of *reme-*

---

[1] See Kuenen's "Hexateuch," p. 4. This unity of purpose, beginning with the Exodus, and running on through the history of Israel, is strikingly set forth in Psalm cxxxvi.

dial grace. To check the downward progress, to provide eventually for the restoration of man to righteousness and life, by sending His own Son to be the Saviour of the world, and meanwhile to separate from the nations of the earth one family, to preserve in that family the knowledge of the One true and Living God by Revelation, and to make them the channel of eventual blessing to the whole human family, was thenceforth the purpose of the Almighty. The sacred Scriptures trace this purpose in successive manifestations to Enoch, to Noah, and then in growing fulness to Abraham, the father of the faithful. And now the Divine counsel begins to take a more distinct shape in the separation of the seed of Abraham to be the chosen people. The purpose of sending the Christ into the world is more distinctly revealed. The family in which the Christ was to be born is more plainly marked out. The birth of Isaac, and of Jacob, and of the twelve Patriarchs, follow in a closely connected chain. The drama advances in the descent of Jacob to Egypt with all his descendants; in the formation of the Israelitish nation during their 200 years residence in Egypt, and then in that grand burst of Divine Power which snapped asunder, like a thread, the iron chains with which Egypt had bound the children of Israel, and sent them forth from the bondage of slaves to the freedom of the greatest nation in the world. It was at this juncture, at the very pivot on which the success of the Divine purpose turned, that Moses was raised up. Moses, the man of God, Moses who towers in the colossal stature of his intellectual and spiritual greatness above all the other Saints and Prophets whose record is in the Book of God. Gigantic alike in his words and in his deeds. Prophet, Confessor, Legislator, Deliverer, Captain of the people. It was the peculiar glory too of Moses, that he not only led the men of his own generation to the knowledge of the Living God, but that he framed those laws and institutions by which they were kept a separate people, "not reckoned among the nations" through some 1300 years, maintaining all the while, in the midst of the idolatries of the great heathen world, the doctrine of the unity of God, and, amidst all the pollutions of heathenism and the foul mythologies of the most civilised nations of the earth, holding forth the light of righteousness, purity, and truth, until the coming of Christ, to establish the yet more excellent system of the everlasting Gospel. Nor were the Mosaic institutions destined to fulfil their purpose without constant hindrances and obstacles. The 200 years, or thereabouts, of their occupation of Canaan in the days of the Judges, put a constant strain upon every joint of the system. The want of a central power to bind the tribes together; the incessant inroads of Philistines, Moabites, and Midianites; and the allurements of the idolatries of the nations around them, would probably have led to the bursting of the bonds of the Mosaic law had they been a whit less strong than they were, and had not the fixed PURPOSE of God supplied the extraordinary aid of the Judges raised up to be the saviours of Israel. And here, in the times of the Judges, the Scriptures bring before us another instrument destined to exercise a great influence on the future destinies of Israel. I mean the instrument of prophecy. Samuel, whose great figure rises up at the close of the age of the Judges, was the first of that long line of prophets who followed one another till it ended in the prophet Malachi. Samuel, David, Nathan, Gad, Iddo, Shemaiah, Elijah, and Elisha, together with those whose writings remain, Isaiah, Jeremiah, Ezekiel, Daniel, Hosea, Joel, Amos, Obadiah, Jonah, Micah, Nahum, Habakkuk, Zephaniah, Haggai, Zechariah, and Malachi, and others whose names are not preserved, form that goodly fellowship of prophets whom God's watchful care for His people raised up from time to time to speak to them the word of the Lord, to rebuke, reprove, and exhort in His Name, and to keep alive the blessed hope of the coming of Christ, and the establishment of His kingdom upon earth. Can the whole world produce any parallel to this? And yet once more. So entirely was this particular people separated to be the people of God, that even their civil government was an object of the Divine care. Saul, their first king, David, the founder of a dynasty which lasted some 500 years, were called to the throne by the express word of God. And the record of the reigns of their other kings down to the Babylonian captivity, has been preserved in the Book of God. And then came the seventy years of exile, and the return of the exiles to their own land under the kings of Persia. Can the whole range of history show anything like this wonderful dispensation? A nation plucked up by the roots and torn away violently from their own land and transported to a distant country, their capital destroyed, their national temple burnt with fire. Kings, priests, nobles, warriors, all carried away captive, and the land left desolate; and yet in less than 100 years the nation reinstated in possession of their ancient country, their temple rebuilt, their priesthood restored, their separate national life resumed, and lasting in completeness and vigour for yet more than 500 years. And then the termination of this Jewish polity, and this Jewish religion, still more wonderful than any other part! The Old Testament running into the New! Jesus Christ the Lord born in David's city, and sitting upon David's throne! Christianity springing out of Judaism, the kingdom of God rising out of the ashes of the Mosaic institutions and the Jewish commonwealth! Thus manifestly do we see the unity of design in Holy Scripture as regards the counsel of God.

(2) View it in the history of the human race. Starting from the creation of man, the Scripture immediately represents the human family, as soon as it begun to multiply, as divided into two classes,—those that feared God, and those that feared him not. Cain and Abel; just Noah and the world of the ungodly; the children of Shem, and the sons of Ham; Abraham and the wicked cities of the plain; Isaac and Jacob, and the Canaanites amongst whom they dwelt, are early examples of this division. It took more definite shape in the later separation of Israel from the nations, and the division of mankind into Jews and Gentiles. The tenth chapter of

Genesis gives a masterly sketch of the divisions of the human family as they sprung from the three sons of Noah, with their various settlements; and Deut. xxxii. 8 has the remarkable statement, that " When the Most High divided to the nations their inheritance, when he separated the sons of Adam, He set the bounds of the people according to the number of the children of Israel." But henceforth the history of those different nations is handled only as far as they came in contact with, and affected Israel. Hence the notices in the Bible of the empires of Egypt, Assyria, Babylon, Persia, as well as of the nations of Canaan, of the Philistines, Edomites, Midianites, and others. I say, then, that to read the Scriptures with intelligence, we must take this unity of design, this continuity of Divine purpose, into account. It is a leading and striking feature in them. And to endeavour to account for the production of those Scriptures by imagining a host of independent writers, some honest, and some dishonest, some speakers of truth, and others disseminators of falsehood, implies a want of perception and appreciation of their true character which is simply amazing, and utterly incapacitates a man for explaining their contents aright. It is as if a man should account for any phænomenon in nature, without any reference to the laws of nature which bind the whole system in one harmonious cosmos, or ascribe the beautiful order of creation to an accidental concurrence of jarring and opposing forces.

But again, if it is true that the selection of Israel from among all the families of mankind to be a peculiar people was the purpose of the wisdom of God, and that all that happened to them through successive ages was the effect of that purpose, and that the Almighty Ruler of the Universe steadily pursued that purpose by successive interpositions of His power, and by the instrumentality of men whom He raised up from time to time, and endowed with special gifts of the Holy Spirit, how can we wonder that critics who absolutely deny that Divine purpose, who exclude the Hand of God from the course of that eventful history, who will have none of revelation, or miracles, or inspiration, or special calling, who put the history of Israel on the same level as that of any other people, and the writers of that history on the same level as any annalist or journalist, how can we wonder, I say, that such critics cannot understand the Scriptures, but only "darken counsel by words without knowledge."

SECONDLY, I would now ask your attention

for a short time to another feature of those Scriptures which are being so ruthlessly handled, and one which does not at all comport with the views of the " Higher Criticism," viz. their marvellous accuracy in a variety of points where mistakes would have been easily made, and where we have it in our power to test their accuracy.

We will take first the very first chapter of the Bible, that which gives us an account of the creation of heaven and earth, and of man, the inhabitant and lord of the earth. Now an account of creation might have been confined to the simple statement of the first verse, "In the beginning God created the heaven and the earth." But it is not so. The first chapter of Genesis tells us certain particulars as to the mode and order of creation. It tells us that this creation was progressive. Heaven and earth did not leap at once into their present condition of order, and their present furniture of light and water and dry land. The present *cosmos* was preceded by *chaos*. The earth was at first without form and void. Darkness was upon the face of the deep. The waters were diffused over the whole earth. But by degrees a change took place. At the bidding of the Creator light shined. The firmament or expanse, or what we now call the sky, environed the earth. As the earth cooled, the waters which formed the sea were gathered into one place, and the dry land appeared. But as yet nothing grew in the earth. The heat made vegetation impossible. Well! thus far I believe the Mosaic account of creation is exactly borne out by the latest results of scientific research and discovery.

But we proceed further. Hitherto we have no life upon the earth, neither vegetable nor animal life, neither fish, nor fowl, nor beast, nor man, such as we see now existing. The Mosaic record goes on to tell us of the creation of these, and of the order in which they were introduced into the earth. (1) There came vegetable life —the grass, the herb, the tree. This was the work of the *third* day. Passing over the fourth day, (2) there came the great swarm of life in the sea and in the air—the fish that move in the sea, and the fowl that fly in the air. This was the work of the *fifth* day. Then (3) the earth brought forth the beasts of the field, the cattle, and all the creeping things that creep upon the earth. This was the work of the *sixth* day. And last of all, at the close of the sixth day, God created man in His own image and likeness— with an intellect, reason, and conscience.

Here then is a definite order of creation. It might have been in any one of 124 different ways. But it is distinctly in the following: Vegetables; fish and fowl; beasts and cattle; man. Now is this the order in which geological science teaches us that these several created things must have been introduced into the earth? or is it not? It is the precise order. In a remarkable letter of the Duke of Argyll's to the *Times* of February 1, 1892, he says: "Alone, I believe, among all the other cosmogonies of the ancient world, it (the Mosaic cosmogony) represents an orderly progression in the creative work. It represents it as work done in time, in stages, and according to a definite sequence of operation." After showing how the description of chaos, and the formation of sea and land, "are in harmony with the latest conclusions on the physical development of a cooling globe," he notices the sequence "vegetable life," "animal life in the sea," "terrestrial fauna later," "man the last and latest creative work, the crown and consummation of the whole," and proceeds: "Mr. Gladstone's assertion is substantially true that the order of the appearance of animals in the first chapter of Genesis has been affirmed in our time by natural science, and may be taken as a demonstrated conclusion, and an established fact." The Duke concludes thus: "Considering its obviously poetic form, and its early date, preceding all that we now understand as science, the depth and extent of its coincidence with all that is as yet known to us, are indeed astonishing." I wonder how the Elohist found it out[1]!

To turn next to the *historical* accuracy of the Scriptures. The Scriptures deal more or less with all the nations and kingdoms of the ancient world. With some it is little more than a casual mention, but with regard to others we have full and copious details of their customs, government, wars, kings, conquests, alliances, and so on. Again, of some of these countries we have considerable knowledge from secular history, but of others, till within the last half or quarter of a century, we had no secular information at all; but within this space of time we have acquired, from monuments and inscriptions and newly-deciphered languages, a great mass of fresh information. The nations with which the Bible brings us in contact are the Egyptians, the Phœnicians, the Assyrians, the Chaldeans, the Hittites, the Elamites, the Philistines, the Moabites, the Edomites, the Midian-

---

[1] The reader will find the same conclusions fully worked out in Dr. Kinn's "Moses and Geology." See also a remarkable paper by Mr. Gladstone in "Home Words," revised in "The Impregnable Rock of Holy Scripture," ch. ii.

ites, the Ishmaelites, the Medes and Persians, the Arameans or Syrians, and many other minor races. Now what a wide field was here for E. or J. or D. or P. while they were writing their "fictitious narratives" about Israel, and their stories "in which there is not one word of truth," to make mistakes in! And yet, strange to say, not one single historical mistake has been detected in all the notices of the nations brought before us in Holy Scripture. Indeed, down to our own times many such notices could not appeal to secular history for support, because there was no extant history bearing upon them. But in the last half century, by the wonderful discoveries and decipherment of the cuneiform inscriptions of Assyria, and the vast increase of our knowledge of Egyptian monuments, a flood of light has been thrown upon many dark pages of ancient history, and in every instance the Bible record has been wonderfully confirmed.

Let us take a very few among many examples of this. In 2 Kings vii. 6 we read of "the kings of the Hittites," coupled with "the kings of the Egyptians"; and in 1 Kings x. 29 we read again of the great traffic in Egyptian horses "for the kings of Syria, and for all the kings of the Hittites" in the days of Solomon. Other notices carry back their existence as a people to the time of Abraham, and represent them later as possessing land as far as the Euphrates (Josh. i. 4). But history was absolutely silent about them. "They had no place in classic history, and therefore it was supposed by some that the Bible references to them could not be true...." "But as soon as the key was found to the Hieroglyphics of Egypt and the cuneiforms of Assyria, a mighty Hittite people began to emerge...." "The increasing light from Egypt and Assyria reveals to us in broad outline and in incidental detail a series of facts with reference to the Hittites in perfect harmony with the narratives of the Bible" (Preface to Dr. Wright's "Empire of the Hittites," pp. viii. ix.). From about the year B.C. 2050 to about B.C. 1320 the Hittites were in constant war with Egypt under the greatest Pharaohs, including Thothmes III and Ramesis II. About the last-named year, shortly before the Exodus, there is a full poetical account from an Egyptian papyrus of a great battle between Ramesis II and the Hittites with 2500 chariots, followed by a treaty of peace which seems to have lasted about 100 years. On the other hand, the Assyrian cuneiform inscriptions tell of constant wars between the kings of Assyria and the Hittites.

From Tiglath-Pileser I (B.C. 1130[1]), for 400 years, there was a constant struggle for supremacy between Assyria and the Hittites, and it is remarkable that there is frequent mention of the number of Hittite chariots. "I took one hundred and twenty chariots fitted to the yoke," says Tiglath-Pileser in his account of a battle with the Hittites. Assur-Nasir-Pal (B.C. 883 to 858) says, "The chariots... of Carchemish (capital of the Hittites) I laid up in my magazines." "The tribute due I received... swift chariots, horses, silver, &c." (p. 40). "Their chariots I took from them" (p. 43). The empire of the Hittites in Asia was not brought to a close till Sargon's final victory over them, B.C. 717 (pp. 43, 44). For further interesting details I must refer you to Dr. Wright's "Empire of the Hittites."

Genesis xiv. 1 supplies another example of very early Biblical records, receiving remarkable confirmation from the latest discoveries of cuneiform texts. This verse smelt strongly of *myth* in the nostrils of critics before the cuneiform inscriptions had revealed their treasures. We now know from the annals of Assur-banipal that an Elamite king, Kudur-Nakhunti, had

---

[1] "Records of the Past," vol. ii. p. 145 note.

carried away a Babylonian image so early as
B.C. 2280; that the Elamites were a warlike
people; that they pushed their conquests into
Phœnicia; that near, or, Lenormant thinks, in
the time of Abraham, they had a king called
Kudur-Mabuk, who had a son named *Eriaku*,
who under his father reigned over *Larsa*—where
we recognize at once the *Arioch* and *Ellasar*
of Gen. xiv. 1. And whether or no Kudur-
mabuk is the same king as Chedor-laomer, we
learn that it was the practice of the Elamite
kings to call themselves by the name of their
favourite idol—Chedor or Kudur, the servant
of—Nakhunti, Mabuk, or La-omer, as the case
might be, just as in the names Nebo-polassar,
Nebuchadnezzar, Bel-shazzar, Merodach-Bala-
dan, &c., the names of the Babylonian gods
Nebo, Bel, and Merodach are contained. With
these discoveries I think we may say that the
smell of myth disappears from Gen. xiv. and
the sweet odour of truth breaks out in its
stead [1].

Another striking example of the confirmation of the historical accuracy of the Scriptures
given by recent discoveries is that in the case
of Belshazzar. It had been a great puzzle to
commentators to explain who the Belshazzar

---

[1] Excursus on Gen. xiv. in Bp. Ellicott's Commentary.

of Daniel v. could be, as secular history (Berosus, quoted by Josephus and Herodotus) tells us distinctly that Nabonidus was king of Babylon at the time of its capture by Cyrus, and that his life was spared by the conqueror, who treated him kindly. The Assyrian cylinders, deciphered by Sir Henry Rawlinson and others, explain the mystery. They tell us that Bel-shar-ussur was Nabonidus' eldest son, that he commanded his armies, and, as appears by other signs, was associated with his father in the kingdom, and was holding Babylon at the time, his father having fled to Sirpar. This explains his offer to Daniel " that he should be the *third* ruler in the kingdom" (Dan. v. 29), Nabonidus being the first, and Belshazzar the second.

Another remarkable instance of the confirmation of an obscure Biblical statement is that afforded by the record "sculptured on the wall of the great temple of El-Karnak" by Sheshank I, king of Egypt. We read in 1 Kings xiv. 25 that "in the fifth year of king Rehoboam Shishak king of Egypt came up against Jerusalem, and took away the treasures of the house of the Lord, and the treasures of the king's house, and all the shields of gold which Solomon had made." The Chronicler (2 Chron. xii.) gives a somewhat fuller account, and specially mentions that "he took the fenced cities that pertained to Judah," v. 4. Shishak's inscription contains a list of places conquered or ruled by him. In this list are seven certain, and many more probable identifications with places in Palestine, of which at least three are named in 2 Chron. xi. 5–10 as having been fortified by Rehoboam ("Dict. of Bible," Shishak).

It would occupy too much time to go at all fully into the history of the wars of the kings of Assyria against the kingdoms of Judah and Israel. It must suffice to state that whereas our knowledge of the kings of Assyria named in the Bible in their relations to the kings of Israel and Judah, derived from secular writers, was extremely scanty, and in some cases a complete blank, the information we have obtained from the newly-opened Assyrian sources about the reigns and wars of such kings as Pul, Shalmaneser, Sargon, Sennacherib, Esar-haddon, agrees in every instance with the brief record in the Bible history. I may add that the illustrations of the history of Hezekiah's reign as given in 1 Kings xviii. xix. are most remarkable. You will find the sculptures relating to the siege of Lachish (2 Kings xix. 8) in Dr. Kinn's interesting volume "Graven in the Rock," where there is also a representation of the cylinder (now in the British Museum) on which the records of Sennacherib's reign are inscribed.

Time will not permit me either to refer to the perfect agreement, now fully brought to light by the large accession to our knowledge of Egyptian papyri and sculptured records, between Egyptian history, manners, customs, laws, &c., and the Mosaic record. But they are a most valuable criterion of the severe historical accuracy of the Pentateuch, to which it is well that your attention should be called.

The next point to which I would draw your attention is the probable SCHEME of the construction of Holy Scripture. I do not think any intelligible scheme can be propounded if we exclude from our consideration the determinate counsel of God that a faithful record of certain events should be kept through all ages for the instruction of His people. The old view of the inspiration of Scripture, as if the whole volume, exactly as we have it now in the Massoretic text, without a clerical error, without a false punctuation, without any exertion of the human will, or the intervention of the industry or intelligence of man in its composition, met this view and was therefore so far satisfactory. But it failed to account for other features of the case, as for instance the different readings from existing Hebrew MSS. and from the old Greek Version called the Septuagint; the existence of a few palpable errors in numbers, proper names, and the like; a few anachronisms such as those I pointed out in my first Lecture; and generally the appearance of a human element in the Scriptures as well as a Divine. And so it exposed the Scriptures to unanswerable assaults from the sceptical school. Moreover, the assignment of the different books of Scripture to particular authors in the same sense as we should mean by a similar assignment, as of the whole Pentateuch to Moses, of the book of Joshua to Joshua, of the books of Samuel to Samuel, of the books of Ezra and Nehemiah to the persons whose names they bear, has in like manner laid the Scriptures open to attacks, which lose all their force immediately the false position is abandoned. What seems to me the true account is, that with a view to effecting His purpose of preserving through all ages a record of certain events, God providentially brought about the recording by the Patriarchs in successive generations of genealogies—the oldest form of history—and of certain events connected with those genealogies—the flood, the destruction of Sodom and Gomorrah, the call of Abraham, and the like—of certain revelations of the Divine will made to those Patriarchs, and ordered the preservation of these records by safe hands. As time advanced, and the Divine purpose of separating a peculiar people to be depositories and guardians of the sacred records approached its completion, and the events which were to bring it about were rising in grandeur and in importance, nothing can be more probable than that such an one as Moses, with his unrivalled opportunities, his splendid powers, his human learning, should be divinely commissioned to gather together and to arrange the ancient patriarchal documents, and to incorporate with them the wonderful narrative of the events in which he played so conspicuous a part, and the laws which he was commissioned to give to the new-born nation. Whether his hand drew up the whole narrative, or it was drawn up in whole or in part by other hands *we are not told*, nor does it in the least matter. But when it was written it was placed in the custody of the Priests (Deut. xxxi. 9, 24-26), to be kept by them for the instruction of the people in all future ages.

In like manner, when under Joshua, the people took possession of Canaan, a faithful record of the event was likewise kept, in part, probably, by Joshua himself, as seems to be indicated by the WE of Josh. v. 1 (*till we were passed over*), in part possibly by others authorized to do so, and then the narrative would be added to the other national archives, and kept under the same authority. When we come to the times of the kings a regular system of historiography was established. We have regular mention of the Book of the Chronicles of the Kings of Israel and Judah, of which apparently the Books of Kings and Chronicles contain extracts ; of "the Book of the acts of Solomon," 1 Kings xi. 41 ; and in David's time we are referred for all his acts, first and last, to "the Book of Samuel the seer, and the Book of Nathan the Prophet, and the Book of Gad the seer" (1 Chron. xxix. 29). That the Prophets continued to write the national records appears from duplicate entries of certain chapters in the writings of Isaiah and Jeremiah, and in the Book of Kings (Isai. xxxvi-xxxix ; 2 Kings xviii. 13–xx. ; Jer. xli. lii. ; 2 Kings xxiv. 18, xxv.). Another indication of the set office of the historiographer may be seen in the regular formula prefixed to the reigns of the Kings. See 2 Sam. v. 4 ; 2 Kings xvi. 2 ; xviii. 2 ; xxi. 5 ; 2 Chron. xii. 13 ; xxi. 8, &c., and in an imperfect state 1 Sam. xiii. 1, where the numerals are not entered, probably because this heading to Saul's reign was inserted much later, when the exact figures were unknown. However, what I wish to suggest is that the earlier annals, those e. g. of the times of Moses, were in their original form probably separate entries—annals of each year, or journals of each day. How far they were arranged by their author we cannot tell. But as time passed on, and they had to be incorporated with subsequent annals, so as to make one continuous history, it is obviously not improbable that some process of editing, arranging, abbreviating, supplying lacunæ, and the like, may have become necessary. Neither is it impossible that in the case of laws an occasional new law or an expansion of an old law may have been added as occasion arose, just as in our own Prayer Book, later additions have been admitted besides the original services of A.D. 1662. But I am far from affirming that this was so.

If the above is anything like the process by which the earlier Scriptures came into shape, it is obvious that these diversities of style, use of particular phrases, prevalence of certain words, and so on, would be fully accounted for without the complicated and cumbrous machinery resorted to by the higher critics. The use of various materials would show itself in the one author—the hand of the late editor would betray itself in its handling of the ancient document. But the suggestion of fraud and dishonesty, or of a patchwork of ingenious and contradictory materials, as the process by which such a book as the Bible came into being, seems to me as destitute of common sense as it is of religious reverence for the Word of God.

Indeed, unless I am wholly blinded by prejudice in favour of Holy Scripture, I see in every page of that wonderful book transparent evidence of the honest truthfulness of the writers. Their words are a genuine coinage stamped with the image and superscription of the God of truth. Literary or other fraud seems to me wholly incompatible with the tone of lofty morality which breathes through those sacred pages. And as to those milder suggestions of the English school of Higher criticism, that in imputing speeches to Moses which never fell from his lips, the writers of Numbers and Deuteronomy were only doing what Thucydides did in putting into the mouths of his great men speeches which represent their sentiments, one has only to look at the particularity with which each separate incident is recorded to see at once how utterly futile, if it were consistent with the respect I feel for some who make it, I should say how *childish*, such an explanation is. Look, e.g., at Num. i. 1, or Deut. i. 3, and numerous similar passages; or such passages as Deut. ii. iii., or Num. xiv., or at the instances in which particular laws sprung up from the incidents of the day, such as the law limiting the marriage of heiresses to their own tribe (Num. xxxvi.); the law prohibiting the use of strong drink by the priest before officiating in the Tabernacle, caused by the offering of strange fire by Nadab and Abihu; the law punishing sabbath-breaking by death, &c., and you will see that there is no choice, no middle way, between deliberate fiction of the most skilful kind, and a genuine document, being what it pretends to be, a contemporary record of real events.

It is not pretended that there are no difficulties to be explained, or, may be to be left unexplained. There are passages in which Moses speaks plainly in the first person, and others in which things are said of Moses which it does not seem probable that he would say of himself —they are more like the narrative of a looker-on. There are discrepancies in the laws, as, e. g., the law of tithes, the different age mentioned as that at which the Levites entered on their service (Num. iv. and viii. 24 [1]), the year of manu-

---

[1] See Kuenen, p. 25 and following.

mission and release from debt, and some others. There are passages, like Deut. x. 6-10, of which it is difficult to say why they are in their present position; and those already alluded to, Deut. ii. 10-12; xx. 20-23; and others. But is it wonderful that a book more than 3000 years old should present certain difficulties? Is it inconceivable that the custodians of the Scriptures should have ever made any blunder? Is our knowledge so extensive that whatever does not exactly fit it must needs be false? By all means let us ever be on the look out for fresh information, but let us mingle a little humility with our curiosity, and not reject solid masses of truth because a few atoms of error or doubt seem to us to be associated with them.

One more general remark and I have done. I began this evening by pointing out the remarkable unity of design running through the Scriptures from the creation to the latest book. I will now ask you to look at the same unity of Scripture from an opposite standpoint. I mean looking backwards from the latest to the earliest books through all the intermediate ones. Each book presupposes those which precedes it. The New Testament presupposes the Old, springs from it, and rests upon it. Malachi presupposes the history of Elijah, the law of Moses, the history of Jacob and Esau. Zechariah presupposes the Feast of Tabernacles, the earthquake in the days of Uzziah, the death of Josiah, king of Judah, the history of David, the Assyrian and Egyptian domination over Israel, and the Babylonish captivity. Haggai presupposes Solomon's Temple, the Exodus from Egypt, and God's covenant with Israel by the hand of Moses (Exod. xxxiv. 27, &c.), and, not to go through all the Prophets, every one of whom presupposes the preceding history of Israel, and bases some part of his exhortation on some special circumstances in it, I may add that the consecutive history of Israel at each stage presupposes what went before. The subsequent reigns look back to David as the founder of the dynasty; the history of David looks back to the history of Samuel (2 Sam. vi.). Samuel presupposes the time of the Judges; Judges (xx. 27, 28) links itself to Joshua in the matter of Phinehas (Judg. xx. 28) and of Jephthah (Judg. xi. 13–26); and the Book of Joshua presupposes the Pentateuch; Deuteronomy presupposes Numbers (Deut. xxiii. 4, 5); Exodus, Leviticus and Numbers all presuppose Genesis in the matter of the tribes, the history of Joseph, the descent of Jacob to Egypt, the history of Abraham, Isaac and Jacob, and so on. So that we have an unbroken chain from

Malachi to Genesis, each link in which bears distinct testimony to all that went before it through, say, 1500 years.

And now I have completed what I had to say preliminary to the direct consideration of the Books of Chronicles. I shall hope in the succeeding Lectures to show you how valuable those Books of Chronicles are in their view of Israelitish history taken from a somewhat different standpoint from the Books of Samuel and Kings, and to establish their authenticity upon firm ground. They will then be invaluable allies in resisting the attacks of a destructive criticism, and maintaining the faith which was once delivered to the Saints, and has been maintained by the Church of God through well nigh 1900 years with unbroken and unfaltering confidence in its absolute and perfect truth.

LECTURE IV.

The Books of Chronicles.

Having at length completed that preliminary examination of the theory of the "Higher Criticism" with regard to the Pentateuch which was necessary to clear the ground, I now proceed to the direct examination of the Books of Chronicles themselves, with a view to establishing their authenticity against the detraction of the "Higher Criticism."

And *first*, let us determine, as far as we can, the age at which the Books of Chronicles were written, and the circumstances under which the people of Israel were placed at the time, and the special wants which the Books were intended to meet.

The *ninth* chapter lets us know at once that we have to do with a post-exilian book. For it speaks, in the first and second verses, of the deportation to Babylon, and of the return from Babylon to their own land of the Israelites, priests, Levites, and Nethinims. How long after the return the Books were written we have to gather from the contents of them, and the latest date to which those contents come down. And since the Book of Ezra is a continuation of the Chronicles, as appears among other things by the three first verses of Ezra being duplicates of the two last verses of 2 Chron. xxxvi., we must take into our account the latest events contained in Ezra, and the latest link in any genealogy contained in either Chronicles or Ezra. Now the history in Ezra comes down to at least B.C. 457, the seventh year of the reign of Artaxerxes Longimanus, king of Persia; and one genealogy, that of Zerubbabel (1 Chron. iii. 19–24), carries us down either six, or more probably three [1], generations after Zerubbabel, which would bring us to about B.C. 446, the twentieth year of Artaxerxes, when we know that Ezra was still at Jerusalem (Neh. viii.). We cannot therefore be very far wrong if we assign the date of the Chronicles to about the middle of the Persian dominion, the time of which the Books of Ezra and Nehemiah treat, the close of the reign of Artaxerxes.

What then was the condition of Israel at that time? There had been two returns of the people from Babylon. The first in the first year of

[1] For the correction of Zerubbabel's genealogy see the writer's "Genealogies of our Lord," p. 97 and following pages.

Cyrus, king of Persia, B.C. 536, under the leadership of Zerubbabel, the heir of David's throne, and Jeshua the high priest. The second in the seventh year of Artaxerxes Longimanus, under the leadership of Ezra the priest, the scribe (B.C. 457). It had been the great work of the first batch to rebuild the Temple at Jerusalem, and this had been accomplished in the course of some twenty years, in the sixth year of Darius Hystaspes, B.C. 515, amidst much opposition from the people of the land. Some progress had also been made with regard to the Temple services. The old divisions of the priests and Levites into courses had been re-established, and the returned captives had kept the Passover. But there is a gap after this in the history of about fifty-eight years, between Ezra vi. 22 and vii. 1. It is likely that after the death of Zerubbabel and Jeshua, and of Haggai and Zechariah the prophets, things retrograded at Jerusalem. There was probably great difficulty in keeping up the Temple services, in finding the requisite number of beasts for sacrifice, and securing the attendance of priests and Levites at Jerusalem. And tidings of this state of things had reached Ezra at Babylon. And so he obtained permission of king Artaxerxes to go to Jerusalem, and also a decree permitting any of the Jewish subjects of the king to go up with Ezra. He also obtained a grant of money from the king, and permission to collect in the province of Babylon free-will offerings, together with an exemption from taxation of all priests, Levites, and Nethinims who ministered at the Temple (Ezra vii. 11–26).

But there was another great evil threatening the destruction of the "feeble Jews" who had returned to Judea, and that was their intercourse with the people of the land, those heathen races whom the kings of Assyria and Babylon had sent to take the place of the Jewish captives who had been exported to Babylonia. It appears from Ezra ix. and x. that many of the Jews, including priests and Levites and chief men of the congregation, had contracted marriages with the people of the land. And later, in Nehemiah's government, there were Jews who had married wives of Ashdod and Moab and Ammon, and their children spake half in the language of their heathen mothers, and could not speak in the Jews' language (Neh. xiii. 23, 24), one of the offenders being grandson to Eliashib the High Priest. Obviously, therefore, there was great danger lest the Jewish race itself, as well as the Jewish religion, should come to an end. It appeared manifestly that the wise institutions of the Mosaic law were absolutely necessary for the maintenance of the separate nationality of the seed of Abraham, as well as for the maintenance of the worship of the One true and Living God. The whole system hung together. The possession of the land according to tribes and families; the genealogies by which the right to possession was secured to each tribe and family; the payment of tithes and offerings by which the priests and Levites were enabled to live at Jerusalem, and keep up the central worship of the Temple; the exclusive spirit of nationality which kept the Jews aloof from all other nations, and the kindred feeling of caste which separated the tribe of Levi from the other tribes of Israel, were all alike needful if Israel was to be maintained as God's witness in the world until the coming of Jesus Christ. Especially important was it that the office of the priests and Levites, which was a fundamental part of the Mosaic system, should be preserved inviolate.

Hence we see the need of a history, for the post-exilian Jews, written in the sense of the Books of Chronicles. The preservation of the ancient genealogies, special record of the part played by the priests and Levites in events already recorded in the national archives, the perils of idolatry, the enmity of the nations, a fuller record of certain passages in their history than had been preserved in the Books of Kings, and which earned for it the name given it in the Greek Version—παραλειπομένων, i. e. supplement or appendix of things passed over in the former history—such were the special features of this last canonical book, which sprung from the wants of the times.

Other peculiar marks of the times in which these books were written, and of the place of their birth, are the following :—

(1) There is little mention of the kingdom of Israel, or of its kings, or of its extinction. By this time the sense of *community* between the people for whom Chronicles were written and the apostate kingdom of Israel was wholly lost. The religious rupture between the kingdom of David and the northern kingdom had produced a complete alienation between the two communities, and this would be felt in its full force by the writers of the *Chronicles*, who were evidently priests or Levites. The affairs of the kingdom of Israel, therefore, are passed over in silence as of little interest to the purely Jewish people for whom Chronicles were written.

Again, if we compare those chapters of Chronicles, which give the account of the closing reigns of the kings of Judah, with the parallel account in the Book of Kings, we shall be struck with the much greater fullness of the narrative in 2 Kings of the reigns of Jehoiakim, Jeconiah, and Zedekiah, as compared with the narrative of 2 Chronicles, and the natural inference will be that the writer of 2 Kings wrote in Judea at the time as we know Jeremiah did, but that the writer of 2 Chronicles did not write at the time. On the other hand, the particularity with which the return of the captives from Babylon under Cyrus is related in the closing verses of 2 Chron. xxxvi. and Ezra i.; Zerubbabel's Chaldee name of Sheshbazzar; the name of Mithredath the Treasurer; the inventory of the gold and silver vessels of the Temple, and the *ipsissima verba* of Cyrus' proclamation; all indicate that the writer was, or had been, a resident at Babylon.

(2) The circumstance, that while the bulk of the book of Ezra is written in Hebrew, from ch. iv. 8 to vi. 18, and ch. vii. 12–26, are in Chaldee, is a strong indication of the time when this part of the narrative was put together, viz. by Ezra himself, or a contemporary, in the reign of Artaxerxes king of Persia.

(3) The mention of Nehemiah the Tirshatha in Ezra ii. 63, and of the sons of Jeshua the son

of Jozadak (Ezra x. 18) brings us down to the same time.

(4) If we include the Book of Nehemiah as well as Ezra, we still do not come below B. C. 432—the thirty-second year of Artaxerxes (Neh. xiii.) or shortly after. We have however one genealogical record (Neh. xii. 11, 22), reaching to Darius Codomanus, B.C. 335, and, v. 23, mention of " the book of Chronicles " as containing entries of Levites down to his reign; his designation " Darius the *Persian*" probably implying that this entry was made under the empire of Alexander the Great. But this does not affect our Chronicles.

SECONDLY. Let us examine the sources—the *Quellen* as our German friends call them—from which the Books of Chronicles are compiled. These are very various. (1) Some are very ancient, evidently drawn from the oldest historical records of Israel. The genealogies which occupy the first nine chapters of 1 Chron. are extracts from the national archives. They are portions of those genealogies according to which the Israelites were distributed by tribes and families in their several inheritances, and in which historical notices were also inserted, as in our Parish registers we often find records of interesting facts. Take a few examples. In 1 Chron. iv. 9 we have a curious mention of Jabez.

The passage is manifestly an extract from some other document, because we do not know who this Jabez was, or who his brethren were. But from the phrase in v. 10, "the God of Israel," it appears that he was *not* an Israelite, and from the names with which he is associated—Kenaz, Othniel, Caleb and others, that he was a Kenezite. And then there is recorded his singular punning prayer, "Oh! that thou wouldest bless me indeed, and enlarge my coast, and that thine hand might be with me and that thou wouldest keep me from evil that it may not *grieve* me!" where he seems to follow up the original saying of his mother when she called his name *Jabez*, "because," said she, "I bare him with *sorrow*," by his own prayer "Keep me from evil that it be not to my *sorrow*," R. V. where the A. V. does not seem to have noticed the allusion to his name, which is apparently the reason why the extract has been preserved. My object is simply to give you an instance of the obvious antiquity of the *sources* of 1 and 2 Chronicles.

Take another curious instance of the preservation of an ancient document, which is in other respects of some importance. I mean that of the Kings of Edom in 1 Chron. i. 43–51, of which a duplicate is in Gen. xxxvi, to which I alluded in my first Lecture. The list is headed,

"These are the kings that reigned in the land of Edom before any king reigned over the children of Israel," and there follows a list of eight kings, which would cover about 240 years. Now the first of these kings was Bela the son of Beor, and his name has clearly some close connection with Balaam the son of Beor, and we know from Num. xx. 14 that there was a king of Edom at that time. On the other hand the last king who preceded Saul was Hadad, and we know that Hadad of the Royal family of Edom escaped as a child from the massacre of Joab and took refuge in Egypt (1 Kings xi. 14 ff.). Here again then we have in this scrap of knowledge preserved in an ancient Edomitish pedigree, evidence of the truthfulness of the chronicler. Supposing Bela the son of Beor to be about contemporary with Balaam the son of Beor, and consequently with Phinehas, we have then exactly the same number of generations from Bela to Hadad inclusive, as from Phinehas to Ahitub, Zadok's father, or, which is the same thing, from the son of Ithamar to Ahijah, who was High Priest in Saul's reign.

Or take the genealogy of a very interesting person, Caleb the son of Jephunneh, of whom we read in Num. xiii.–xv. It there appears that he was one of the twelve spies who were sent to search the land, one for each tribe, and each one a head or ruler of his tribe, and that he was for the tribe of Judah. On their return from the land bringing the grapes of Eshcol with them, you will remember that Caleb and Joshua were the only two who brought a good report, and encouraged the people to go up and take possession. The other spies gave such an evil report of the fenced cities, and the huge stature of the sons of Anak, that the heart of the people melted with fear, and they rose up in rebellion against Moses and Aaron, and were on the point of stoning them, and making a captain to return to Egypt. As a punishment for this rebellion, the Lord declared that none of the grown-up men of that generation should enter into the promised land, except Caleb the son of Jephunneh and Joshua the son of Nun (Num. xiv. 30). And accordingly in Josh. xiv. we read how Caleb the *son of Jephunneh* the Kenezite came to Joshua, reminded him of Moses' promise, and asked to be allowed to drive out the sons of Anak from the mountain, and take possession of it. "And Joshua blessed him, and gave unto Caleb the son of Jephunneh Hebron for an inheritance." Hebron therefore became the inheritance of Caleb the son of Jephunneh the Kenezite unto this day, "because that he wholly followed the Lord God of Israel" (Josh. xiv. 14). Now in 1 Chron. ii. we have Caleb's genealogy, derived from Judah through Hezron, agreeing with Joshua xv. 13, "Unto Caleb the son of Jephunneh he gave a part among the children of Judah." On the other hand we have no clue to who Jephunneh was. Nor again have we any clue to the personality of Kenaz, from whom he is called the *Kenezite*. But a careful examination of the names in the Edomitish genealogies reveals the fact that Kenaz (1 Chron. i. 36, 53) is an Edomitish name, and the names Shobal, Reaziah, the Manahathites, Korah, Temani, Elah, are all common to the Edomitish families, and to the descendants of Caleb. Putting all this together we get this consistent story, that Caleb was not an Israelite at all, but had attached himself to the children of Israel, and so had obtained an inheritance with the children of Judah, as a reward of his faithfulness to the Lord God of Israel, having also doubtless married into the tribe of Judah. I submit that "fictitious genealogies" do not bring out such results.

Other little touches of history are not only full of interest, but bear the strongest possible marks of genuineness and truth. Among the rare notices of the tribe of Simeon is that of their raid upon the pastures on the east side of the valley of Gedor, and the utter destruction of a certain Hamite population of shepherds who had their tents there, and the appropriation of the rich pastures to their own use. This expedition seems to have been followed up by another farther to the south, to Mount Seir, and by the destruction of the remnant of the Amalekites who dwelt there. And this information was derived from some documents compiled in the reign of Hezekiah, the time when these things happened (1 Chron. iv. 39-43). Or look at the account in 1 Chron. v. of the war carried on by the Reubenites against the Hagarites in the days of Saul, their great victory and slaughter of their enemies, their immense capture of cattle, 50,000 camels, 250,000 sheep, 2000 asses, and their expansion as far as the wilderness bounded by the river Euphrates. And this information, we gather, was gained from the genealogies drawn up in the reigns of Jotham, king of Judah, and Jeroboam II, king of Israel (1 Chron. iv. 19).

Or look at the exceedingly ancient story which the genealogy of Joshua the son of Nun, of the tribe of Ephraim, brings us (1 Chron. vii. 20 ff.) There a bloody contest with the men of Gath, caused as usual by a raid for cattle, in which it does not appear clearly who was the

aggressor, issued in a terrible slaughter of the
Ephraimites, and a touching account is given
of the grief caused to the head of the tribe by
this calamity. There is a good deal of obscurity
in the account, and doubt as to the precise time
when the events took place; but whether the
slaughter of the Ephraimites took place before
or after the entrance into Canaan, it is a
manifestly genuine extract from a very ancient
document, and seems to be extracted from a
genealogy drawn up in the time of Joshua.

Many more interesting scraps of history not
mentioned elsewhere are scattered amongst
these genealogies. But I will only advert now
to another class of entry, I mean the notices of
certain trades which came under the genealogical divisions of the land. Thus 1 Chron. ii.
55 we read of "the families of the scribes which
dwelt at Jabez"; 1 Chron. iv. 14 of "Joab the
father of the valley of Charashim (craftsmen),
for they were craftsmen"; at 1 Chron. iv. 21 of
"the families of the house of them that
wrought fine linen, of the house of Ashbea."
Ver. 23 of the same chapter tells us of "the
potters, and those that dwelt among plants and
hedges: there they dwelt with the king for his
work." Little scraps of knowledge, these,
mingled with an occasional census of certain

tribes, or an occasional mention of an Assyrian invader, Pul, or Tilgath Pilneser, which show us what an interesting collection the whole must have been, and what rich materials it contained for a social and statistical history of the twelve tribes of Israel.

I turn next to an indication of the genuineness of the Chronicles, which strikes me as of great weight as showing that they are copies of the original documents. You will doubtless have observed in reading many of the genealogies, which form so important a portion of these books, that they are of very various lengths, and break off at very various times, the reason of which is not at first sight very clear. But a very simple, I had almost said a very obvious reason, is that the genealogy transcribed breaks off necessarily at the time when it was made— a genealogy drawn up in the reign of David could not go beyond the reign of David. One drawn up in the reign of Hezekiah could not go beyond the reign of Hezekiah. A genealogy drawn up in the reign of Jotham king of Judah, or Jeroboam king of Israel, would of course end with the generation contemporary with those kings respectively (1 Chron. v. 19). But we have not always the means of knowing in what reign the last person in any list lived, because he may be an utterly unknown person. But sometimes we have. Take for instance the genealogy in 1 Chron. ii. 25–41. It is a genealogy of the tribe of Judah, viz. of the descendants of Jerahmeel the son of Hezron, the son of Pharez, the son of Judah, for twenty generations. In it are two names that we know, names i. e. of persons of whom we know when they lived. One is Zabad of the 14th generation after Judah, whom we recognize at once as David's mighty man *Zabad the son of Ahlai* (1 Chron. xi. 41) by the designation "the son of Ahlai." *Ahlai* being the name of Sheshan's daughter who married her father's Egyptian servant Jarha, and so gave her name to that branch of the family. Reckoning four more generations from Zabad in David's reign, brings us down to *Azariah*, whom we identify at once as the Azariah son of Obed of 2 Chron. xxiii. 1 in Athaliah's reign, by his being the grandson of Obed. Five more generations bring us to the end of the list. But if we reckon the number of generations from David to Jehoram, Athaliah's husband, we find six, corresponding to the four in the line of Azariah— a perfectly satisfactory agreement, if you consider that Zabad, the last of the mighty men, was probably a full generation younger than David, and that Azariah may well have been an older man by near a generation than Jehoram who died at the age of forty (2 Chron. xxi. 20). Lastly, from Azariah to Elishama, the last name on the list, there are six names, and in the line of kings there are six kings from Athaliah to Hezekiah. We may be pretty sure therefore that Elishama lived in the time of Hezekiah; but we know also that Hezekiah had a great staff of scribes (1 Chron. iv. 41; Prov. xxv. 1). Hence we conclude that the last name in the pedigree indicates that the genealogy was drawn up in Hezekiah's reign, and as a threefold coincidence, Zabad, the 14th from Judah, is in his right place as David's contemporary; Azariah is in his right place as contemporary with King Jehoram; Elishama is in his right place as contemporary with Hezekiah's scribes.

Another example of the termination of a genealogy in Hezekiah's reign is that in 1 Chron. viii. 34–40, where from Jonathan the son of Saul to Ulam are eleven generations, corresponding to the eleven generations between David and King Hezekiah.

An analogous indication of these genealogies being transcripts of original genealogical tables may be found in the different accounts they give of the same tribe at different times. Take e. g. the tribe of Benjamin; we have four different accounts of the families or houses into which the tribe was divided (1) as it was when Jacob went down into Egypt (Gen. xlvi. 21); (2) as it was at the entrance into Canaan (Num. xxvi. 41); (3) as it was in the days of David; (4) as it was in the days of Hezekiah (1 Chron. viii), where you may observe another indication of the historical character of these genealogies in the greatly diminished numbers of the tribe from 45,600 (Num. xxvi. 41) to 22,034 (1 Chron. vii. 7), showing the desolating effect on the tribe of Benjamin of the great civil war in the time of the Judges.

Or we may test the historical accuracy of the genealogies of the Chronicles on a much larger scale, and in a manner which would not have been possible fifty years ago. When I was writing my little book on the genealogies of our Lord some forty years ago, I had occasion to examine as carefully as I could the chronology of the portion of time between the Exodus and David. And I found that while in our Saviour's genealogy there were only *five* persons, —Salmon, Boaz, Obed, Jesse, David—to fill up the gap between the Exodus and the Kingdom of David, the time, according to the received chronology, to be accounted for was from 480 to 600 or even more years. It did not require to be a conjurer to see that these two conditions did not harmonize. I set to work therefore and read all the best books on the chronology of the times, Jackson, Hales, &c., to get the difficulty cleared up. One solved the difficulty after one sort, and others after another. One learned man thought he had solved the difficulty when he routed up the record of old Parr, who lived to be 152 years old, and so might have had a son at over 100 years, and therefore why should not four or five in succession do the same? But the most part, thinking the received chronology, founded partly on the Biblical chronology in 1 Kings vi. 1; Judg. xi. 26, &c., and partly upon Egyptian chronology, to be incontestably true, resorted to the not unreasonable expedient of supposing the genealogy to be defective, some of the links being left out, and only the principal names inserted. And this explanation might have sufficed if we had only one genealogy to deal with. But, upon looking carefully into the genealogies covering this particular period of time, it appeared that there were no fewer than *eight* other genealogies covering the same interval of time. In five of these there are fourteen generations, in two fifteen, and in one eleven, corresponding with the eleven in David's line.

Hence it was manifest that the contradiction between the chronology and the genealogy was not to be accounted for by supposing some of the links in the genealogical chain to be missing. My own conviction therefore was that it was the chronology which was at fault. I was greatly confirmed in this conviction by a passage in Sir Gardner Wilkinson's "Manners and Customs of the Egyptians," vol. i p. 99, in which he states that while he acquiesces in the then received opinion that Thothmes III. was the Pharaoh of the Exodus, he thinks Lord Prudhoes' view that *Mene-phthah*, who lived nearly 200 years later, was the Pharaoh of the Exodus is well worth consideration. The difficulty in the way of accepting it was that it brought down the Exodus about 200 years too late, that is to just the time indicated by the genealogies in the Books of Chronicles. My book was not out of the printer's hands when Dr. Lepsius' (the great Prussian Egyptologer) Letters from Egypt appeared, in which he argues with great force from the Egyptian point of view that Mene-phthah was the Pharaoh of the Exodus, shows how this brings the date of the Exodus 178 years later than the common date (and so 178 years nearer to the time of David), and adds " that the Scripture genealogies, the *only trustworthy although less exact chronological thread* of those Hebrew times, speak as decidedly against the calculation hitherto adopted of 480 years (from the Exodus to the building of Solomon's Temple) as in favour of . . . about 300 years." Well this was nearly forty years ago, and these forty years have been a time of unexampled progress in the study of Egyptian antiquities, and the knowledge of ancient Egyptian history. And what has been the effect of this increase of knowledge upon the question of the Exodus? Why that every Egyptologist of any note now agrees that Mene-phthah is the Pharaoh of the Exodus, and that the Exodus took place nearly 200 years later than the old chronologies had supposed!

Now is it not most remarkable that the genealogies in the Chronicles should exactly bear out what is thus discovered to be the truth? Can you conceive "fictitious genealogies" to be thus in harmony with those ancient Egyptian monuments which are now revealing the secrets of 3000 years ago? Does it raise, or does it *lower*, your estimate of that omniscient higher criticism which professes to find out, not by the light of history, not by the light of newly discovered documents, not by the revelation of newly deciphered languages, but by the light of their own searching intelligence, what happened and what did not happen 3000 years ago, and do not scruple to brand as the work of deceivers and forgers books which 100 generations of faithful men, before and after Christ, have unanimously accepted as the scriptures of truth? When you see that these men are not clear-sighted enough to see the broad marks of truth stamped upon these records, because those marks are destructive of their theories, can you give them credit for that marvellous keenness of mental vision which enables them to break up the text of scripture into a perfect mosaic of E's and J's, and D's, and P's, and R's, contradicting one another, and yet making up the most sublime, the most beautiful, the most harmonious, the most instructive volume which the world has ever seen, and which amidst all the glories of Greek and Latin literature, and all the wisdom of Eastern sages, and all the wealth of Western learning and civilization, still holds its place, unrivalled, and unapproached, as the Bible, the Word of God?

I had forgotten specially to remind you that several of these genealogies are those genealogies of High Priests and Levites which our omniscient friends have informed us were invented by the Priests of the fourth century before Christ to support the fiction of an Aaronic

Priesthood, and a central altar of sacrifice, and to secure the payment of tithes for their own personal emolument.

(2) But to proceed with the sources. Besides those ancient genealogical rolls which we have just considered, and the existence of which proves the preservation of the national records through the Captivity, the following works are quoted by the chronicler as used by him in compiling his work. For the reign of David he had the Book of Samuel the seer, and the Book of Nathan the Prophet, and the Book of Gad the seer: abundant materials of the most authentic kind. What portion of the existing Chronicles could have been derived from the Book of Samuel does not clearly appear, seeing it does not begin till after Samuel's death. But possibly at one time much which we now read in 1 Sam. may have been attached to the beginning of the Books of Chronicles, and afterwards omitted, as not required in duplicate. Or, without supposing this, it may be that some of the arrangements for the services of the Levites which were afterwards adopted by David were originated by Samuel, as seems to be suggested 1 Chron. ix. 22. See too 1 Chron. xxvii. 28. From the Book of Nathan the Prophet he probably derived those particulars about the preparation of materials for building

the Temple which are not found in 2 Sam. (1 Chron. xxviii., xxix.), and those details concerning the building which are not in 1 Kings. From the Book of Gad he would derive the accounts of the musical services of the Levites which are scattered through the Books (1 Chron. xvi. 4-6; xxv. 1-6; xxiii. 5, &c.), as we gather from the statement in 2 Chron. xxix. 25.

The chronicler also refers for the acts of Solomon to "the Prophecy of Ahijah the Shilonite" of whom we read 1 Kings xi. 29, 2 Chron. x. 15, and to "the visions of Iddo the seer" (2 Chron. ix. 29, and xii. 15); for the acts of Rehoboam to Shemaiah the prophet (2 Chron. xii. 15); for the acts of Abijah to another work of Iddo the prophet (2 Chron. xiii. 22); for the reign of Jehoshaphat "to the book of Jehu the son of Hanani" (2 Chron. xx. 34). For the reign of Joash a book is referred to called the "story of the Book of the Kings" (2 Chron. xxiv. 27); and for the reign of Uzziah we are referred to Isaiah the prophet (2 Chron. xxvi. 22). The reign of Hezekiah is also vouched for by "the visions of Isaiah the son of Amoz" and "the Book of the Kings of Judah and Israel" (2 Chron. xxxii. 33). For the reign of Manasseh we are referred to a book called דִּבְרֵי חוֹזָי, "the sayings of the seers" or "the history of Hosai."

Besides the above authorities the compiler of Chronicles refers frequently under slightly varying forms to "the Book of the Kings of Israel and Judah" (1 Chron. ix. 1; 2 Chron. xxiv. 29); that is, I conceive, the official annals of the kingdom constantly cited in the Book of Kings, as the Book of the Chronicles of the Kings of Israel or Judah (1 Kings xiv. 29 ; xv. 7 ; xv. 31 ; xvi. 20, &c.); so that he had the most authentic contemporary authority for the whole course of his history down to the Captivity, and appears to have been most painstaking and conscientious in his use of the authorities at his disposal. How far he used our present books of Samuel and Kings is difficult to determine; because, though we have many consecutive verses identically the same in Chronicles as those which we read in Samuel and Kings, we cannot be sure whether the author took them from our present books or from those official annals to which they both so frequently refer. I propose in my next Lecture examining more closely the relations between the Books of Chronicles and those of Samuel and Kings which precede them, when perhaps we shall be able to arive at some definite conclusion. Coming down to the close of the Chronicles, and the commencement of Ezra, we have a gap of over fifty years, except so far as it is filled by the

Prophets Ezekiel and Daniel, and by the brief statement of 2 Chron. xxxvi. 20. But at 2 Chron. xxxvi. 22 the thread is taken up again, and we find ourselves at the same point of time as we touched at 1 Chron. ix. 1, viz. the return of the captives from Babylon. Here then the continuity of the history is resumed. Ezra i.-vi. relates the return of the Jews from Babylon under the leadership of Zerubbabel of the House of David and Jeshua the High Priest, and the Prophets Haggai and Zechariah; the rebuilding of the Temple under the constant opposition of the people of the land; the celebration of the feasts of Tabernacles and of the Passover, and the gradual restoration of the Temple services. Besides the direct narrative of the Book of Ezra (which is the continuation of 2 Chron.) we have too the Prophecies of Haggai and Zechariah relating to the same time, and bearing distinct evidence to the hereditary High Priesthood and to the existence of the law. Then follows another gap of about seventy years. And then at last Ezra himself appears upon the stage, having come up from Babylon in the seventh year of Artaxerxes Longimanus. But I will ask you to notice particularly that the great progress toward the resuscitation of the law of Moses recorded in the first six chapters of Ezra; the restoration of the Holy Vessels, brought from Jerusalem to Babylon by Nebuchadnezzar (ch. i); the building of the altar of the God of Israel to offer thereon burnt-offerings, as it is written in the law of Moses the Man of God (iii. 2); the keeping of the Feast of Tabernacles and the other set feasts (iii. 4, 5); the ordering of the ministry of Priests and Levites, with trumpets and cymbals and singing after the ordinance of David king of Israel (iii. 9–11); and the rebuilding of the Temple (v. vi.); had all taken place some seventy years before Ezra came to Jerusalem, and between eighty and ninety years before Nehemiah came. But no doubt, with the Prophets Haggai and Zechariah on the spot, and Zerubbabel and Jeshua at the head of the civil and ecclesiastical establishments, official Chronicles were kept of the transactions of that period. And these are the authority, probably to a great extent the very words, of the first six chapters of Ezra. But that we have not those official Chronicles exactly as they were left by their authors, and as Ezra found them, is certain, because ch. ii. is a duplicate of Neh. vii. and iv. 6–23 relate to Xerxes and Artaxerxes who reigned after, not before Darius, and relate not to the building of the Temple, but to the walls of the city, which was the great work Nehemiah accomplished.

With Ezra vii. then, which is a manifest continuation of the preceding narrative, we have introduced the authority of Ezra himself, an eye-witness of all that he relates. For from Ezra vii. 1 to ix. 14 is written in the first person, and Ezra x. is also probably by his hand, though Ezra is spoken of in the third person. Whether Ezra himself edited the book that bears his name with the preceding Chronicles, as we now have them, or some later editor incorporated Ezra's work with the Chronicles, and added Nehemiah's, is difficult to decide, and at all events need not detain us now.

I have concluded now all I have to say as to the *sources*—the *Quellen*—of the Books of Chronicles. And I hope I have shown you that they are of the most trustworthy kind. Original documents, in many cases of great antiquity, and contemporary authorities for the whole of the time dealt with, together with internal evidence of the suitability of the book to the wants of the times and the circumstances under which it purports to have been published, and internal evidence also of the genuineness of the documents appealed to, have I think shown us that as a whole the Books may be thoroughly trusted, and may be absolutely acquitted of the gross dishonesty and fraud imputed to them by the "Higher Criticism."

In my next, concluding Lecture, I shall put them to the further test of a close comparison with the Books of Samuel and Kings; and shall then in conclusion show that they offer an uncompromising and insuperable contradiction to that audacious tenet of the higher criticism, that the law of Moses is the fiction of a late age and that the Pentateuch had no existence till Moses had slumbered many centuries in his grave.

LECTURE V.

CONCLUSIVE TESTIMONY OF CHRONICLES TO THE MOSAIC LAW.

Our first task this evening is to examine somewhat closely the relations of the Books of Chronicles to the Books of Samuel and Kings, with a view to discover whether, in the light of such a scrutiny, they sustain the twofold character of an *independent* history, and an *authentic trustworthy* history. The facts of the case are these. From 1 Chr. x. 1 to 2 Chr. xxxvi. 21 we have a history of Israel running parallel to that which begins 1 Samuel xxxi. 1, and ends 2 Kings xxv. 30. In what do these histories agree, and in what do they differ? Where Chronicles differ, do they contradict Kings? Where they agree, are they merely a servile echo of Kings? And what are the main features of difference?

Perhaps the clearest way of bringing out these different points will be to take different sections of the history and compare the treatment of them by the two books, one with another. And we will take *first* the reign of David.

If we place 1 Chr. x. 1–12 by the side of 1 Samuel xxxi. we see at once that, with one or two slight verbal differences, they are *verbatim* the same account, either copied the one from the other, or both borrowed from a common source. Again, 1 Chr. x. 13, 14 exhibits at once what we shall see is a peculiarity of the chronicler, viz. to moralize on the facts which he narrates. His comment on the death of Saul is "So Saul died for his transgression which he committed against the Lord, . . . and for asking counsel of one that had a familiar spirit to inquire of it, ... therefore He slew him, and turned the kingdom unto David the son of Jesse." Similar comments recur frequently (2 Chr. xii. 2, 7, 12; xiii. 18; xiv. 6, 7; xvi. 8, &c.). If we pass on to 1 Chr. xi. 1–9, and compare it with 2 Samuel v. 1–10, we find ourselves again on identical ground, the accession of all the tribes to David at Hebron, and the capture of the stronghold of Jebus, the castle of Zion, which is the city of David. With slight variations the two accounts are identical, either transcripts of the same passage, word for word, or one the copy of the other. But all the account of the civil war between David and Ishbosheth, and the murder of Abner, and of Ishbosheth, which occupies the intermediate chapters of 2 Samuel (i–iv.), is omitted in Chronicles.

Advancing to 1 Chr. xi. 10, and proceeding as far as xii. 30, we notice the chronicler's familiarity with statistics, and official lists. For we have a long list of David's mighty men and their valiant deeds, and another of those tribes which joined David at Ziklag; and yet another of those who joined him at Hebron, to make him king, down to the end of ch. xii. And it was to this assembly that David proposed bringing up the ark to Jerusalem (2 Samuel vi. 1). The appearance is of a reference to official records; but we are struck at the same time with a feature which we shall have to consider again, viz. of excessive numbers beyond the bounds of probability. If we reckon up the numbers of the armed bands who came to David at Hebron, as given in the last half of ch. xii., we find they mount to 309,600. And it is added that they all feasted together three days, eating and drinking with David. But to feast 300,000 men for three days is no easy task. Now it so happens that in this particular case we have the numbers given in the parallel passage, 2 Samuel vi. 1, on a much more manageable scale, 30,000. And this also suggests an easy correction of the numerals here and elsewhere. In Hebrew numerals were often expressed by single letters. Thus ג stands for three; ל for 30, ש for 300, each ׳ having the effect of multiplying by ten. If, therefore, in the original list the sum total, 30,000, was expressed by a *gimel* (for three) and one dash, and with the word for *thousand* following it, the accidental addition of one dash by a careless scribe would at once convert 30,000 into 300,000, and big numerals flattering the vanity of the Jews, what was at first a clerical error would become the *textus receptus*, like the impossible 50,070 of 1 Samuel vi. 19.

The next event recorded is the important one of bringing the ark from Kirjath-jearim to Jerusalem. The ark seems to have been at Kirjath-jearim ever since it had been brought there from Beth-shemesh (1 Samuel vii.), after its restoration by the Philistines. The two accounts in many respects agree verbally, and are clearly derived from the same source. The ancient name of Baal given to Kirjath-jearim, the description of the ark as "the ark of God that dwelleth between the Cherubims," the mention of the instruments of music, the names of Abinadab, Uzzah, Ahio, Obed-edom, the incidents of the new cart, the stumbling of the oxen, the name Perez-Uzzah given to the place to commemorate Uzzah's death, and the turning aside of the ark into the house of Obed-Edom the Gittite, are decisive proofs of the two narratives being derived from the same source. But even in this part of the narrative there are several indications of the chronicler having drawn from other sources as well. The way the subject is introduced in 1 Chron. xiii. 1, 2, 3 ; the mention of " Priests and Levites in their cities and suburbs," and the description of the land of Israel as extending from " Shihor of Egypt unto the entering of Hamath," indicate that the chronicler had some other account before him, or possibly the same account from which 2 Sam. was taken, but taken with much less abbreviation.

But with regard to the latter part of the narrative the difference between the two accounts is very marked. First, whereas in 2 Samuel vi. the whole narrative of bringing up the ark to Jerusalem is given consecutively, 1 Chron. xiii. only brings the account down to the lodging of the ark in the house of Obed-Edom, and then interposes the chapter about Hiram, and David's sons born at Jerusalem, and the battle with the Philistines at Baal-perazim, and in the valley of Rephaim, which corresponds with the latter half of 2 Sam. v. And then chapter xv. 1 supplies information not given at all in 2 Sam., viz. that during the three months that the ark was resting at the house of Obed-Edom, David was making preparations at Jerusalem for the due reception of the ark. He pitched for it a tent, and apparently the houses which he built in the city of David (1 Chron. xv. 1.) were for the Priests and Levites who were to have charge of it. For as appears from 1 Chron. xv. 29 and 1 Kings xiii. 1, the Tabernacle prepared for the ark was in the city of David. And then there follow all the details of the preparations made for assembling the Priests and Levites at Jerusalem, for assigning to them their respective parts as bearers of the ark upon their shoulders "as Moses commanded," as singers, with instruments of music, as blowers with trumpets, and as porters or doorkeepers: details not one word of which are given in the parallel account in 2 Sam. vi., but which must all have existed in fact, and are implied in the narrative in 2 Sam. vi. And then the narrative in Chronicles at xv. 25 rejoins that in 2 Sam. v. 12, telling with it, though in somewhat abridged terms, of the progress of the ark from the house of Obed-Edom to the city of David, of the sacrifices offered on the way, of David dancing before the ark clothed in a robe of white linen, and a linen ephod, of Michal,

Saul's daughter, despising him in her heart, and of the distribution of bread and meat and wine among the people. Omitting the further incident of Michal's reproach to David and David's answer (2 Sam. vi. 20-23) the chronicler proceeds with the matter which specially interested him, the permanent provision made by David for Levites and Priests to minister before the ark—settling them, I presume, in the houses which he had built on Zion. It is interesting, with reference to the strange theories broached about the Psalms, to notice that the special office of some of these Levites was " to record, and to thank, and to praise the God of Israel with psalteries and harps," and that the chapter closes with several Psalms said to have been given by David at that time for the service of praise into the hands of Asaph and his brethren, viz. the 106th, 1-15; xlvi.; lvi.

Passing on to 1 Chron. xvii. and xviii., we find them, with scarce an exception, verbally the same as 2 Sam. vii. and viii. But the incident of David's enquiry after the house of Saul, the restoration of Saul's land to Mephibosheth the son of Jonathan, and the taking of him to eat at the king's table continually, which forms the subject of 2 Sam. ix., is wholly omitted in Chronicles.

The next event in David's life is his war with Hanun the son of Nahash, the king of the children of Ammon. This is related in identical terms in 2 Sam. x. and 1 Chron. xix., down to the time when the Syrian kings made peace with David, and broke up their alliance with the Ammonites. The issue too of the war in the capture of Rabbah, and the taking the crown of the king of Ammon and putting it on David's head, is related mostly in identical words in 1 Chron. xx. 1–3, and 2 Sam. xi. 1, and xii. 26–31. But all the events which cast so dark a shadow on this part of David's life, and which are related in the Book of Samuel with such unsparing fidelity, the adultery with Bath-sheba, the death of Uriah, the troubles in his family, the rebellion of Absalom, the flight of David, in short the whole contents of 2 Sam. xi.–xxiii. (except that the lists of the mighty men in 1 Sam. xxiii. had been already given in 1 Chron. xi., and the battles with the Philistines in 2 Sam. xxi. 15–22 are given in 1 Chron. xx. 4–8) are wholly omitted in Chronicles. And then both the books meet again in the account of the numbering of the people, and the building of the altar on the threshing-floor of Araunah the Jebusite. The two accounts are on the whole identical, but bear very much the appearance in one or two places of being drawn from a common source, but differently abridged or altered by the two parties. Thus what in 2 Sam. xxiv. occupies verses 5, 6, 7, 8, in 1 Chron. xxi. is condensed into the statement in half verse 4, "Joab departed, and went throughout all Israel, and came to Jerusalem." While the statement in 1 Chron. xxi. 6, "Levi and Benjamin counted he not among them: for the king's word was abominable to Joab," is not found in 2 Sam. at all, though it is again alluded to 1 Chron. xxvii. 24, with a reference to "the chronicles of king David."

So again the statement which in 2 Sam. xxiv. is condensed into the last verse of the chapter, in 1 Chron. xx. fills the last five verses, 26–30, with the additional important statement about the Tabernacle of the congregation at Gibeon, confirming the statement of 1 Chron. xvi. 39, and 1 Kings iii. 4.

This is exactly what would have happened, if the two writers, having a common document before them, had each put in or left out particular portions according as it suited the main purpose of their history.

The First Book of Kings opens with the account of the last illness of David, the intrigue of Adonijah to secure the succession to the throne for himself, the anointing of Solomon to be king by David's order, his riding through the city on the king's mule, David's last charge and counsel to Solomon, and David's death, 1 Kings ii. 10, 11. That is, the whole of what is related of David's reign subsequent to the numbering is comprised in one and a half chapters. But in 1 Chronicles there follow eight chapters. Yet we do not seem to meet on any common ground till we come to 1 Chr. xxix., second half of verse 22, in which, and the following six verses, the whole contents of 1 Kings i.-ii. 11 are condensed—the only passages of verbal agreement being 1 Chr. xxix. 26, 27, and 1 Kings ii. 11, 12.

What then are the contents of these closing chapters of 1 Chron.? They relate almost exclusively to David's preparation for the building of the Temple by Solomon, and for the due conduct of the Temple services after it was built. It had been related in 2 Sam. viii., as well as in identical words in 1 Chron. xvii., that David's express desire to build a temple for the Lord had been rejected because he had been a man of war and had shed much blood (1 Chron. xxviii. 3), but that God had promised him that Solomon his son should build a House for God's Name. It was a natural sequel to this that David should make great preparations, and collect materials fitted for the magnificence of the House which was to be built. Accordingly, as soon as the preliminary step of bringing up the ark of the covenant from Kirjath-jearim to the city of David had been accomplished, and a site had been purchased of Araunah the Jebusite, David set to work to make all the necessary preparations, and the history of these preparations is what engrosses the attention of the chronicler through the remainder of the annals of the reign of King David, the source of his information being doubtless "the chronicles of King David" (xxvii. 24). These preparations were of a manifold character.

(1) He charged Solomon his son to undertake the work, exhorting him to obey the law of Moses, and promising him prosperity by God's blessing if he did so (1 Chron. xxii. 6-16; xxviii.).

(2) He commanded all the princes of Israel to help Solomon in the great work of building the House to the Name of the Lord (xxii. 17-19; xxix.).

(3) He collected the offerings of the whole congregation, and joined with them in a solemn service of prayer and praise (chapter xxix.).

(4) He collected a vast treasure from his own private property, from the dedicated spoils of war, and from the national treasure at his

disposal, of gold and silver and brass, and cedar wood, and iron and stone; he secured a goodly gang of hewers of wood from Tyre, and workers in stone, and he called out for forced labour the strangers, i.e. the old Canaanite inhabitants throughout the land (xxii. 2).

(5) Having thus made provision for the fabric, David's statesmanlike and organising mind proceeded further to make provision for the orderly conduct of the various services of the Temple. As a skilled musician himself he had a high conception of the part music, both vocal and instrumental, ought to play, in showing forth the praises of God, and in emphasizing those Psalms and Hymns and spiritual songs of which he himself was such a skilled composer. As a musician, too, he well knew the importance of numbers practising together if they would attain to excellence. And then there were the other ministries to be performed " for the service of the House of the Lord, in the courts, and in the chambers, and in the purifying of all holy things, and in the work of the service of the House of God: both for the show-bread, and for the fine flour for the meat-offering, and for the unleavened cakes, ... and to offer all burnt sacrifices unto the Lord in the Sabbaths, in the new moons, and on the set feasts by number,

according to the order commanded unto them...
and that they should keep the charge of the
tabernacle of the congregation, and the charge
of the sons of Aaron in the service of the House
of the Lord" (xxiii. 28–32), and accordingly he
caused all the Levites to be numbered from the
age of thirty years and upwards, even 38,000.
Their services were thus distributed. Twenty-
four thousand men for the service of the House
of the Lord; six thousand were officers and
judges; four thousand were porters or gate-
keepers of the various gates of the Temple; and
four thousand formed the skilled choir of vocal
and instrumental musicians set apart to praise
the Lord. But of course this large number did
not act in their respective offices simultaneously.
Being first broken up genealogically into families
and houses, each under their respective heads,
they were thus, both Priests and Levites, distributed into courses, and their order of succession
in their courses was decided by lot. Thus ch.
xxiv. tells us of the twenty-four courses of the
Priests, sixteen of the house of Eleazar, and
eight of the sons of Ithamar; ch. xxv. tells
us of the twenty-four courses of Levites whose
office it was to praise with harps and psalteries
and song; ch. xxvi tells us of the divisions
of the porters. These all attended in rotation,

apparently (1 Chron. xxvii. 1) a month at a time, or perhaps in some cases a week at a time (2 Chron. xxii. 4). And so doubtless the other divisions of the Levites had each their turn of waiting on the active discharge of their duty at the Temple, and when their waiting was over went to their own homes in their several cities and suburbs.

To convey this information concerning David's preparations for the Temple was I conceive the main object of the chronicler in these chapters; and that he derived his information from "the chronicles of David" I think there can be no doubt, both from the mention of them in 1 Chron. xxvii. 24, and from the nature of the entries preserved in these last chapters. But it was very natural that, having been led to record these particulars in reference to the Temple, he should add a few more details of general interest. Such are the twelve courses, each under its own captain, and each consisting of 24,000, into which the whole kingdom was divided for doing the king's business, and probably forming the militia of the kingdom (1 Chron. xxvii.), the interesting information that this census took place in the fortieth year of David's reign (xxxvi. 31, 32); the mention of the spoils won in the battle by Samuel, and Saul, and David, and Abner, and Joab, and others, and dedicated by them, and placed in the Lord's treasury under the hand of Shelomith the Levite, and his brethren (1 Chron. xxvi.); the curious information in ch. xxvii. about the officers who had the charge of all the king's property, his treasurer, the keeper of his store-houses in the fields, in the cities, in the villages and in the castles; his chief bailiff over all his farm-labourers; the manager of his vineyards, the manager of his cellars of wine, and those of oil, the keeper of his olive trees and sycamore trees, the several chief-shepherds of his divers herds and flocks, the master of his camels and of his asses (he had no horses), and the names of his secretary, of his counsellor, of the governor of his sons, of his companion, and of the general of his army. I say it was very natural for one who like the chronicler had a manifest interest in statistical documents to throw in these very interesting details, though they did not bear directly upon the main object which he had in view, viz. David's preparation for the building of the Temple.

But I will ask you to notice in passing what a strong evidence these details of the civil administration bear to the fact that this census, taken in the fortieth year of David, is the source of the important notices of Priests and Levites, and other institutions of the law of Moses contained in the Chronicles. Interesting as these notices are in themselves, it strikes me that their greatest value is the strong contradiction which they offer to the offensive suggestion, that these and all the references to Mosaic laws and institutions are the impostures of a late age, and of a designing and interested priesthood.

And now to sum up the results of the survey we have taken of the two histories of the reign of David.

I feel justified in affirming with perfect confidence that the chronicler is both an independent and a trustworthy historian. He is not a mere copyist of the pages of Samuel and Kings, and he is not a romancer and fable-writer when he parts company from them. He drew his information from authentic sources, and original documents. Widely as he diverges in his history of David from the writers of Samuel and Kings, he never contradicts them. But as the main purpose of his history was different from theirs, it necessarily happens that he often omits what they insert, and inserts what they omit, and that he abridges when they write in full, and enters into details when they cut a matter short. Speaking generally the Books of Chronicles give the ecclesiastical history of David's reign, the Books of Samuel and Kings give the civil history.

II. The same is true of Solomon's reign. If we compare the account of the dedication of Solomon's Temple in 2 Chron. v. vi. vii. with that in 1 Kings viii. though there is perfect harmony in the two accounts, and that in Kings makes distinct mention of the ark of the Lord and the Tabernacle of the Congregation—which the "Higher Criticism" informs us did not exist for more than 500 years afterwards—and of the Priests and Levites, yet we shall notice the much greater fullness of detail with which the chronicler describes the action of the Levites, the presence of *all* the Priests—not those only whose course fell on that day—the music sung, the dress of the Levites, the instruments of music, and the worship of the people (2 Chron. v. 11–13 as compared with 1 Kings viii. 11). It is an ecclesiastical mind that is speaking, one deeply impressed with holy things, one wishing to impress his readers with the vital importance of maintaining in full vigour the religious ordinances which they had inherited from their fathers, and had lately so wonderfully recovered. Any signs of fraud or fiction I have failed to discover.

Occasionally, indeed, the account of secular matters is given more fully in Chronicles than in Kings, as, for instance, the account of the invasion of Shishak, King of Egypt, is given more fully in 2 Chron. xii. 2-9, than in 1 Kings xiv. 25, 26, which is evidently owing to the chronicler having before him the book of Shemaiah the Prophet (2 Chron. xii 7, 15); a full account is given of the invasion of Judah by Zerah the Ethiopian, Shishak's successor, in the days of Asa, which is wholly omitted in Kings (2 Chron. xiv. xv.); and so in some other cases: but usually, as in 2 Chron. xiii. in the account of the war between Abijah and Jeroboam; in 2 Chron. xvii. in the account of Jehoshaphat's reign; and elsewhere, the details which are given in Chronicles, but not in Kings, are of an ecclesiastical and Levitical character.

III. It would take too much time to verify this by a comparison of all the reigns. But it will fall in with my general design of exhibiting the different method of the two histories to compare their treatment of two other reigns, those of Joash and of Hezekiah. In the account of the restoration of Joash, the little king, and the deposition and death of the usurper Athaliah, the writer of Kings makes mention only of the rulers over hundreds, and "the captains and the guards," i. e. the king's body-guard—the royal troops who were now revolting from Athaliah—and whose duty it was to be in the courts of the Temple for the protection of the sovereign (2 Chron. xii. 11); and he relates how Jehoiada the High Priest arranged that when they relieved guard on the Sabbath the outgoing guard should remain, and with the incoming guard should occupy certain posts, and also guard the King's person; but he makes no mention of the Levites (2 Kings xi.).

On the other hand the chronicler (2 Chron. xxiii.) relates that Jehoiada on that Sabbath did not as usual dismiss the courses of Priests and Levites, but retained the outgoing with the incoming courses, and distributed them to guard certain posts, and also as body guards to protect the person of the little king. But he does not speak specially of the king's guards. But in the first verse he does make special mention of certain captains of hundreds, one of whom was our old friend Azariah, the son of Obed, entering into covenant with Jehoiada, and of many chief men from Judah joining the conspiracy, and of Jehoiada arming the captain of hundreds with spears and shields and bucklers, which David had put in the House of the Lord; and of the princes (verse 13), and of the captains of hundreds (verse 14). So that the chronicler's account does not in any wise clash with that of Kings, but is simply silent with respect to the guards, while the writer of Kings is silent about the Levites. But it stands to reason that the same expedient of retaining the outgoing with the incoming forces must have been applied both to guards and Levites.

The clause in 2 Kings xii. 18 which says, "And the Priest appointed officers (offices Heb.) over the House of the Lord," in 2 Chron. xxiii. 18 runs thus, "Also Jehoiada appointed the offices of the House of the Lord by the hand of the Priests the Levites, whom David had distributed in the House of the Lord, to offer the burnt-offerings of the Lord, as it is written in the law of Moses, with rejoicing and with singing, as it was ordained by David. And he set the porters at the gates of the House of the Lord, that none who was unclean in anything should enter in": where you see the Levitical mind dwelling upon the ceremonial details, but not a vestige of fraud or deceit. What the chronicler records in detail agrees exactly with what the writer of Kings sets down in brief.

A comparison of the two accounts of the collection of money for the repair of the Temple, and of the repairs themselves, presents some curious features. They agree in all main points, in blaming the Priests and Levites for the delay, in recording the actual restoration of the fabric, and the part taken by the king, the High Priest, and people respectively; but there is less appearance than usual of the narrative being derived from a common source. A very important allusion to Leviticus in 2 Kings xii. 16 is not made in 2 Chron.; though on the other hand we see the usual *animus* of the chronicler in the special mention of the action of the Levites, and the identification of the collection with that ordered by Moses for the Tabernacle of witness (2 Chron. xxiv. 6). The chronicler also alone gives us the information that the sons of Athaliah had wilfully broken up the House of God, and bestowed its treasures upon Baalim.

But the most striking difference between the two histories of the reign of Joash consists in the total suppression in the book of Kings of the apostasy of Joash after the death of Jehoiada, and the King's base ingratitude in the murder of Zechariah the son of Jehoiada—referred to by our Saviour in Luke xi. 51. But this is hinted at in 2 Kings xii. 2, which tells us that " Joash did that which was right in the sight of the Lord *all his days wherein Jehoiada the priest instructed him,"* implying that after Jehoiada's death he ceased to do so, as expressly stated in 2 Chron. xxiv. 17, 18. So that here again we have proof that the chronicler is an independent and also a trustworthy historian.

We turn next to the reign of Hezekiah. In 2 Kings xviii. we have this record of him: "He did that which was right in the sight of the Lord according to all that his father did. He removed the High Places, and brake the images, and cut down the groves, and brake in pieces the brazen serpent that Moses had made . . . He trusted in the Lord God of Israel, so that after him was none like him among all the kings of Judah, nor any that were before him. For he clave to the Lord, and departed not from following Him, but kept His commandments which the Lord commanded Moses." And then the sacred historian passes immediately to the secular affairs of the kingdom; Hezekiah's rebellion against the King of Assyria, his victory over the Philistines, then the destruction of Samaria, and the captivity of the northern kingdom. Then he goes on to the invasion of Judah by Sennacherib, and the memorable destruction of Sennacherib's army; and closes with Hezekiah's sickness, and the visit of the ambassadors of the King of Babylon. But he says not one word about the ecclesiastical affairs of the kingdom.

On the other hand the chronicler (2 Chron. xxix. ff.), after telling us in identical language with 2 Kings xviii. 3, that " He did that which was right in the sight of the Lord according to all that David his father had done," plunges at once into the history of Hezekiah's ecclesiastical reforms. He tells us that in his very first year he began the restoration and purification of the Temple which had been profaned. He gives the King's stirring address to the Priests and Levites, narrates how zealously they responded, how they cleansed the House, and the altar, and all the vessels which Ahaz in his transgression had cast away. Then he tells us of the sacrifices which they offered up to make reconciliation, of the restoration of the Levitical services of song and musical instruments according to the commandment of David, and Nathan the Prophet, and Gad the King's seer; that the people brought such a multitude of burnt offerings that there were not priests enough to flay them till more Priests had sanctified themselves. And then in ch. xxx. gives a detailed and glowing account of the great Passover—adding at the end " So there was great joy in Jerusalem: for since the time of Solomon the son of David

King of Israel, there was not the like in Jerusalem." He then goes on in ch. xxxi. to detail Hezekiah's other ecclesiastical reforms: the destruction of all idolatrous objects, altars, groves and the like; the restoration of the courses of Priests and Levites, for the service of the Temple; the appointment of the King's portion of his substance for the regular sacrifices, and of the people's portion of tithes and offerings for the maintenance of the Priests and Levites; he describes with enthusiasm the liberality of the people, and the abundance of first-fruits, of corn, wine, and oil, and honey, and of the increase of the field, as well as the tithe of oxen and sheep; he then gives the names of the principal officers of the Levites who had the charge of all these things " at the commandment of Hezekiah the King, and Azariah the Ruler of the House of God," i. e. as described in verse 10, "Azariah the chief Priest of the House of Zadok." He then mentions how the Levites from three years old and upwards, and also the Priests, according to their genealogies, received their portions from the offerings of the people, and concludes " thus did Hezekiah . . . and wrought that which is good and right and truth, before the Lord his God. And in every work that he began in the service of the House of God, and in the law, and in the commandments, to seek his God, he did it with all his heart, and prospered." And then, having given eighty-four verses to the ecclesiastical history of Hezekiah's reign, he closes it with thirty-three verses on the great secular events of the reign, an abridged account of the invasion of Sennacherib, and the destruction of his army, a brief allusion to Hezekiah's illness, and to the ambassadors of the King of Babylon, and a glowing description of Hezekiah's wealth and prosperity; and, with only one discordant note of blame for his pride in the matter of the Babylonish ambassador, he consigns him to an honoured grave in the chiefest of the sepulchres of the sons of King David. Brief, however, as the chronicler's account of Sennacherib's invasion is, he manages to give some interesting particulars concerning the defence of Jerusalem, and the supplies of water during the siege, which are not given in 2 Kings xviii. (2 Chr. xxxii. 2-8).

Again, then, as the result of our scrutiny of the chronicler's account of the reign of Hezekiah, as compared with that in the Book of Kings, I affirm boldly that his character as an independent and trustworthy historian is thereby established. That his mention of ceremonies and divers ecclesiastical matters which are not mentioned in Kings is perfectly natural, and does not even excite suspicion ; and that the charges brought against him by the " Higher Criticism," of wilfully inventing things in order to bolster up the fiction of the law of Moses, are false and calumnious, and, not resting upon any solid foundation, are unworthy of scholars and critics.

With regard to the few passages in which contradictions are alleged to exist between Kings and Chronicles, this is hardly the fit time to go into them at any length. I will only observe generally that the omission by one writer of things inserted by another is no disagreement. Both writers have manifestly abridged the common account they had before them, one in one place, and another in another, according to the special object each had in view. And we know that the omission of one circumstance in a chain of events will often give an appearance of contradiction which the missing fact immediately removes. The most remarkable omission is that in 2 Kings xxi. where no mention whatever is made of the deportation to Babylon of Manasseh, or of his repentance and restoration, and of his buildings at Jerusalem after his return—all which are related at large in 2 Chr. xxxiii. It is perhaps worthy of mention that whereas the writer of 2 Kings

xxi. 17 refers for his authority to "the Book of the Chronicles of the Kings of Judah," the chronicler refers, in addition to the "Chronicles," to a book called "the sayings of the seers." The apparent discrepancies in the account of the Temple, and the collection of the funds in the reign of Joash, are in any case trivial, and in all probability are not real. The disagreement, at first sight more serious, in the account of Ahaziah's death in 2 Kings ix. 27 ff. and 2 Chron. xxii. 7 ff., disappears entirely when we perceive that the account in Kings is very much abridged, and that there is a gap of a day or two between the first and last parts of 2 Kings ix. 27, allowance for which brings the narrative into perfect agreement with the fuller account in Chronicles. Ahaziah was not slain on his flight from Jezreel the same day that Joram was, as we should infer if we had only 2 Kings ix. 27 to guide us, but on his flight from Samaria, where he had been hiding, towards Megiddo [1], and just after the slaughter of his brethren to whom (and not to Joram) the *also* in verse 27 refers.

[1] If, as seems probable, the "Garden House" (Beth-Gan. Heb.) 2 Kings ix. 27, is the same place as En-Gannim, now Jenim, it is on the direct road from Jezreel to Samaria, and so this verse confirms the statement in 2 Chron. xxii. 9, that Ahaziah escaped in the first instance to Samaria.

One word with regard to the enormous numbers in the Books of Chronicles, which is the only substantial charge I can see against the accuracy of the chronicler. It must be confessed that such numbers as " 500,000 chosen men of Israel" slain in one battle (2 Chron. xiii. 17), Asa's army of 580,000 men (2 Chron. xiv. 8), Zerah the Ethiopian's host of a million men, and 300 chariots (verse 9); Jehoshaphat's army of 1,160,000 men (2 Chron. xvii.), the 120,000 valiant men of Judah slain in one day by Pekah, and the 200,000 men and women taken captive at the same time; and possibly some others, besides the 300,000, which I referred to at the beginning of my lecture, of those who met David at Hebron, are incredible numbers. I think the most probable explanation is, that which I have suggested before, that they originated in clerical errors caused by the method of expressing numerals by letters, and perpetuated by the vanity of the copyists who liked big numbers. There are two causes of clerical errors in regard to numbers. One is the resemblance of certain Hebrew letters to one another. For instance ב (beth) and כ (caph) are continually mistaken for one another in MSS. But ב as a numeral means 2, כ means 70. The letters ד (daleth) and ר (resh) are scarcely distinguishable from each other; but *daleth* as a numeral means 4, while *resh* means 200. The other is, what I explained above, the habit of expressing 30, 300, 3000 and so on by the number of little dashes appended to the letter expressing *three*, and so with other numerals. I do not give this as a *certain*, but only as a possible explanation of what seem to be impossible numbers.

And now, in conclusion, having as I hope vindicated the character of the Books of Chronicles, and established their claim to be honest witnesses and faithful historians, it only remains to point out how absolutely destructive of the theory of the "Higher Criticism" as to the law of Moses their testimony is. Indeed the advocates of that theory are well aware of this, and hence their efforts to discredit the Chronicles. Just as a counsel in a law-suit, who knows that the evidence of one of the witnesses is fatal to the cause of his client, does everything in his power to blacken the character of that witness, and show that his evidence is not worthy of credit.

The contention of the "Higher Criticism" is, you will recollect, that the law of Moses is really of post-exilian origin, that it had no existence during the ages of the Judges, and the Kings of

Israel and Judah; that the Pentateuch instead of being of the age of Moses is the work in part of the time of Josiah, and in part of the days after the return of the captivity from Babylon, viz. the days of Ezra and Nehemiah; that the hereditary High Priesthood of the descendants of Aaron is a post-exilian fiction; that the separation of the tribe of Levi for an exclusive ministry is a fiction; that there was no such thing as the Tabernacle of witness or one altar of sacrifice, but in the imagination of P, with other like assertions. Well! we have gone through the reigns of twenty-one Kings of Judah from David to Zedekiah. In David's reign we have found the most elaborate organisation of Priests and Levites for the service of God exactly according to the Mosaic ritual; we have seen most solemn ceremonial for placing the Tabernacle of the congregation and the ark of the covenant, and the one altar of sacrifice on God's Holy Hill, and frequent reference to the law of Moses as the standard aimed at. Among genealogies, proved in the most striking manner to be genuine, we have seen the descent of the High Priests of both lines deduced from Aaron, and the historical High Priests all falling in their right place. In the reign of Solomon we have seen the building of the Temple, and everything still in accordance in all their details with the law of Moses and the Levitical institutions. Passing over other reigns, where the same truth might have been brought out still more strongly, we came to the reigns of Joash and of Hezekiah, and saw precisely the same institutions existing as an essential part of the life of the nation. Passing on to the times after the return from Babylon we saw, in our fourth lecture, how the returned exiles struggled to restore the Mosaic institutions—rebuilt the Temple, restored the courses of Priests and Levites, celebrated the feasts of Tabernacles and of the Passover, and that several scores of years before the return of Ezra and Nehemiah. How is this compatible with the non-existence of the law of Moses, and the Levitical order during those 600 years?

Or put it in another way. The Tabernacle of witness (or tent of meeting) is mentioned something over eighty times in the Pentateuch, in which it occupies a most conspicuous place. In each of the historical books which follow the Pentateuch, viz. Joshua, Judges, 1 Samuel, 2 Samuel, 1 Kings, 2 Kings, 1 Chronicles 2 Chronicles, it is mentioned once or more, in all about eighteen times. How is this compatible with the non-existence of the tabernacle till after the time when these historical books were written?

The Pentateuch tells us very impressively that God bestowed the hereditary High Priesthood upon Aaron and his sons. And we have given us in the Chronicles a genealogy of High Priests beginning with Aaron, and ending with Jaddua, containing twenty-nine generations. Of these we meet incidentally in the course of the history (outside the Pentateuch), viz. in the Books of Joshua, Judges, 1 and 2 Samuel, 1 and 2 Kings, 1 and 2 Chronicles, Ezra and Nehemiah, each turning up in his right chronological place, nineteen filling the great office of High Priest. How is this compatible with the non-existence of an Aaronic Priesthood?

The Pentateuch in most vivid colours describes the institution and celebration of the first Passover, with reiterated provision for its perpetual celebration as a memorial of the deliverance of the children of Israel. We saw in our second lecture that in the historical books (outside the Pentateuch), viz. in Joshua, 2 Kings, 2 Chronicles, and Ezra, there is a detailed account of the celebration of four Passovers, with clear hints of several other celebrations. How is this compatible with the theory that the law enacting the Passover is posterior to all these recorded celebrations of it?

The Pentateuch records the separation of the tribe of Levi for a special ministry, and assigns them a livelihood from the tithes and offerings of the other tribes. The historical books in all subsequent ages exhibit this tribe in positions agreeing with this separation. In consequence of it we are told that they had no inheritance of land allotted to them as the other tribes had. The entire history of this wonderful people bristles with notices of these Levites, their functions, their ministry, their various offices. The genealogies are full of them. We know their divisions and sub-divisions into families and houses of fathers, better than we know our own. The names of their great musicians— Heman, Asaph, Jeduthun, are as familiar to us as the Mozarts and Beethovens of our own times. We know the families who returned from Babylon, who took part in the restoration of the Temple service in virtue of their office, 2400 years ago. We know by name as familiarly as we know our own Tyndales and Latimers the Levites who helped forward Hezekiah's great reformation, and those who were the coadjutors of the good Josiah; and now at the bidding of Messrs. Wellhausen and Kuenen we are to believe that the Levites were never set apart at all, that their consecration was a fiction, their origin and office a myth. We are bid take a sponge and wipe out with remorseless cruelty all that history and geography and poetry have taught us of the most wonderful race of men the earth has ever seen. The great record of God's dealings with mankind, upon which our own hope of good things to come is founded, is to be put on the shelf with *Aesop's Fables* and the *Lays of Ancient Rome*, and the *Arabian Nights*: the very teaching of our Lord Himself, the faithful and true Witness, is to be discredited, and we are to believe what the "Higher Criticism" of to-day is pleased to teach us, leaving it to our children to believe in the "Higher Criticism" of to-morrow, and to our grand-children to be involved in the darkness and gloom of an universal scepticism.

My friends, my reason rises up in revolt at the claims of this unreasonable criticism, and my faith shudders at the surrender it is called upon to make of its allegiance to the authority of our Lord Jesus Christ. And when I have put together as carefully as I can all the facts of the case, and have weighed, as fairly and impartially as I can, all the considerations which the "Higher Criticism" brings before us, I only return with greatly increased confidence to the ancient faith, and to an implicit reliance upon the truth of Holy Scripture as given by Inspiration of God.

If anything that has been said in the course of these Lectures shall have helped you to retain the same happy conviction, by showing you how groundless are the arguments of the "Higher Criticism," and, to borrow the words of a great statesman, how impregnable is the Rock of Holy Scripture, I devoutly thank Almighty God, and rejoice that now that I am cut off from other activities I have had this opportunity of speaking to you on one of the most momentous subjects of the day.

Gloria Patri, et Filio, et Spiritui Sancto,
Sicut erat in principio, et nunc, et in saecula saeculorum.
Amen.

www.ingramcontent.com/pod-product-compliance
Lightning Source LLC
Chambersburg PA
CBHW022112160426
43197CB00009B/993